Not What You Had Planned

NOT WHAT YOU HAD PLANNED

Finding Strength and Hope in the Storms of Adversity

ROBERT B. HAASE

Burton Press International — Olympia, Washington

Burton Press International
Attention: Permissions Coordinator
1910 4th Ave E Unit 234
Olympia, WA 98506

Note: The names of the people who are written about in this book have been changed to protect their privacy, unless otherwise noted.

ISBN 978-1-7351710-0-5 (Paperback)
ISBN 978-1-7351710-1-2 (Kindle eBook)
ISBN 978-1-7351710-2-9 (Audio Book)
ISBN 978-1-7351710-3-6 (Hard cover)

Cover design by Burton Press International.
Cover image: © Arcady www.fotosearch.com

Printed in the United States of America
Published by Burton Press International

www.notwhatyouhadplanned.org

"When we are no longer able to change a situation – we are challenged to change ourselves."

– Viktor Frankl[1]

---

[1] Frankl, V. E., (1959) Man's Search for Meaning, Boston, Massachusetts: Beacon Press

TABLE OF CONTENTS

ACKNOWLEDGMENTS

I want to thank my wife, Teran, for supporting me in this book project even as we were continuing to face adversities ourselves. Thank you for your encouragement, baby.

I am thankful for my daughters, Ashley, Sara, and Holly, for being my inspiration, purpose, and reason not to give up when I was at my lowest point. My hope is that they never have to draw upon my example of resilience when they face inevitable adversities during their lifetimes.

I want to thank those who've helped and encouraged me in the writing and editing process, and for offering critical feedback on the manuscript for this book, including Lori Holbrook, Josh Mercer, Lisa McAlpine, Matt Brost, Pam McKinnie, Denisa Anderson, Suzanne Olson, Marilyn Hunter, Denise Moffat, Lisa D'Hondt, and Jim Ladd.

To my proofreader, Olivia Toy, thank you for your attention to detail and for helping to make sure the manuscript was ready for press.

And to my editor, Susan Alexander, thank you for your diligent work to help shape this book into a message of hope.

Lastly, I want to thank those who were brave enough to share the details of their very personal stories of adversity with me.

INTRODUCTION

It was the infamous year of 2008 when I was proud to have achieved a most noteworthy, personal trifecta of adversity: My wife left me, I lost my business, and I was diagnosed with cancer. Also, having guaranteed all my business loans personally, I was forced to file bankruptcy, so I lost my home and car as well.

Now fast-forward to 2014.

In those six years I had endured a total of fifteen surgeries and biopsies. I also had lost the entire left half of my tongue, and I had survived a traumatic near-death experience as well as cancer treatment.

One summer weekend while still healing from surgery and subsequent chemo and radiation treatments, I drove my parents down to the tranquil seaside Oregon town of Mazanita to attend a family reunion. After arriving and greeting everyone with hugs and small talk, family members dispersed themselves throughout the beach house and its surrounding property, chatting and catching up in small groups. It wasn't long before I found myself on the sofa in a quiet conversation with my mother's cousin, Judy.

Judy had been a brilliant educational consultant in her career but, sadly, was now in the early stages of dementia. As we talked, I couldn't help but notice how she had lost her sharpness. But suddenly, as dementia patients often do, Judy had a moment of clarity. She looked me in the eyes, and with a genuine interest and a gentle smile, she asked me, "Aren't you proud, Bobby?"

Unsure of what she meant, I asked, "Proud of what?"

"Proud that you made it through this whole experience!" she replied with a look of wonder on her face.

"Actually," I responded, "I did what anyone would do. I didn't have a choice! If you were in a house that was fully engulfed in flames and you saw an open door on the other side of the flames, you would run through those flames to get through that door."

Judy grasped my hand and held it. "Don't you know that many others would have sat down in those flames and given up? *You didn't!* You chose to fight, and you made it through!"

Judy's words seemed to reverberate through me as though everything and everyone in the house froze in time. Thinking back over the chain of events which had led to that moment felt like I had been shaken awake from a dream only to realize all of it really happened. My choice hadn't been so much to *fight,* but simply to refuse giving up as an option. I had a reason to live. *Three* reasons, actually. I had to make it through for my three daughters.

Something happened to me that day. I started to have an

unquenchable desire to encourage others who—like me—had been facing adversity in their own lives, and to give tools and hope to the family members and friends who had been supporting them.

Overwhelmed with my vision, I embarked on my mission to write a book. I began gathering blog posts and notes from my personal journals, and I thought about what my objectives would be. What were my basic message and purpose?

Through that important thought process, two truths became increasingly clear to me:

- *Everyone* faces adversity in some form during their lifetime.

- If I am going to write a book, it has to explore beyond my own journey and reflect on the adversity others had endured, how they made it through, what they learned from it, and what wisdom they would want to share with others.

Now, six more years have passed and I am about to publish that book I once only dreamed about. More than ever, I believe the insights learned by people who have emerged from adversity can change you. I believe their stories of loss, hope, and courage will leave you better equipped to face any adversity which comes your way with increased resolve, resilience, faith, and confidence. And, if you are the one supporting a friend or family member through their own adversity, I believe you will gain critical insights into how to give them the support and encouragement they need.

The analogy of choosing to *run through the fire* to escape a burning house is the same for each of us. Each type of adversity we encounter is a *burning house* of sorts, and how we react to a situation is a choice nobody can make for us. My hope is that from reading this book, you will join me in making the choice to *Run Through the Fire.*

Access free resources, information, and news related to this book at www.notwhatyouhadplanned.org.

CHAPTER ONE
Life Before the Storm

It was just after midnight, sometime in the fall of 1989, when, unable to sleep, I got out of bed, made my way into the front room of our condo, eased back into my favorite recliner, and flipped on the television. Our baby daughter was sound asleep down the hall, and her mother was finally asleep as well. I found myself aimlessly channel-surfing as I repeatedly pressed the channel button on the remote. Finally, I ended up on the classic movie channel. The old black and white film was nearly over, but for some reason, I paused.

The scene was a posh, downtown men's club sometime in the 1930s. Two men were holding a conversation while lying face down on adjacent massage tables, each with his own muscle-bound therapist. With their khaki slacks, white tee-shirts, and shaved heads, both practitioners looked like Mr. Clean. I watched, mesmerized, as they pummeled the tension out of the men's bodies as if kneading raw bread dough. I was intrigued at the thought of using one's hands to help others out of their pain.

At the time, I was a busy and successful project manager for a large commercial construction company. My job involved meeting with companies who wished to expand or build a new building. I helped design the proposed structure, provided a competitive bid, closed the sale, and then followed the job through until we handed the customers their keys. I was good at my job—really good. But I had grown bored and no longer felt that commercial construction was my calling.

Within a few days, I had done a little research, picked a starting point, and contacted the Brian Utting School of Massage in nearby Seattle. I enrolled in their one-day introductory workshop and scheduled a tour.

The school was in an old two-story brick building about a half-mile from the Space Needle. I guessed it was either intentional retro-grunge-chic or just a run-down old property awaiting gentrification. Either way, it had a memorable character, with exposed wood beams and electrical conduit, brick walls which had been shabbily patched up over the years, creaky wooden stairs whose sturdiness I wouldn't bet my life on, and live plants everywhere. In fact, live foliage seemed to be growing in any available spot, from the first-floor entrance to the second-floor offices. I could hear soft, new-age music wafting through the building and there was a familiar earthy smell suggesting a combination of incense, scented candles, patchouli oil, and dank, old library books.

Great. Hippies, I remember thinking to myself with a moderate measure of disdain.

After my interview and tour of the school with Marlene, the admissions director, I decided this school wouldn't be a good fit for me. It was probably great for free-thinking bohemian types, but that wasn't me. I was a *yuppie*. I had arrived in a pressed white shirt, wool crepe slacks, and a swanky silk tie, driving a new Volvo 740 Turbo with one of those cool, built-in cell phones—the handheld kind with the thick, black, curly cord that stretched from the phone to the dash.

Furthermore, Marlene had provided me with an uninspiring brochure that had been primitively formatted on an old Macintosh computer, printed in black ink on plain white paper, and stapled at the corner. I was not impressed.

Nevertheless, still believing a career in massage therapy might be the right path for me, I decided to stick with it and took the school's one-day introductory workshop. By the end of the class, it had become even more clear: I was simply captivated at the thought of being a massage therapist.

The trouble was it was 1989, and I was more than aware that massage was far from a mainstream profession. It was definitely more of a hippie thing—surely not a serious career choice.

But the feeling didn't subside, and I thought of little else over the next few days. Finally, I shared with my wife that I was thinking about giving up my frantic and unfulfilling Bellevue-Redmond commuter's life to go back to school and become a massage therapist—a career which likely wouldn't pay even half of what I had been earning.

Logically, I wasn't expecting much enthusiasm for the idea. With Debbie staying home to raise was our toddler, I was the sole breadwinner. So, I was more than surprised when Debbie simply said, "Okay."

Next, it was time to tell my parents, so the following weekend we invited them to come for dinner. After we finished eating, we moved our conversation into the living room while 18-month-old Ashley happily sat in her highchair, coloring. Both Mom and Dad had looks of anticipation on their faces when I took a deep breath, and said rather abruptly, "We have something to talk to you about..."

It's essential to understand how my parents had regarded my career track up to that point. Back in junior high, I had been an ambitious, money-making paperboy. In high school, I was senior class president and voted most likely to succeed. I had landed every job I had applied for throughout high school and college, had earned a B.A. from a respected four-year university, and was currently working for a highly regarded company which rewarded me handsomely for my work. Understandably, my parents' expectations were high. I prepared myself for the looks of disappointment which would surely appear on their faces after hearing my news.

Leaning forward with my hands clasped together and elbows resting on my knees, I looked up, alternately looking into their eyes, and said nervously, "I've been thinking about changing my career. I've not been happy for a while, and even though I am good at what I do, I don't *enjoy* what I do. I cannot see myself continuing in a job that isn't fulfilling, so I have decided to go back to school to become a licensed massage therapist."

Much to my surprise, my father's face formed a gentle, re-assuring smile with knowing, comforting eyes, the familiar half-squint he'd always had when about to say something important.

"Bob, I've been an accountant for the past thirty years," he said to me. "Even though it has supported our family, I've dreaded every minute of it. If you've found something that interests you, go for it. Do what makes you happy."

I will never forget those words. I was stunned. On the one hand, my parents were apprehensive about my giving up the security of such a good position. On the other hand, they had always believed in me and knew I could thrive in whatever I put my mind to, including becoming a massage therapist.

And that was that. I took a leap of faith, quit my unsatisfying job, and enrolled in the Brian Utting School of Massage. Choosing to put my education and future in the hands of people who weren't like me *at all* probably seemed counterintuitive to others. I didn't care about how my decision may have looked from an outside perspective. It didn't matter. I wanted to be challenged.

Brian, who owned the school, had a reputation for being somewhat of a non-conformist, but from a business standpoint, he was brilliant. We shared the same perfectionistic personality, which I knew would make the difference in the education I would receive. Was the school *flashy?* Not in the least. Did his graduates have a reputation for being exceptional? *Absolutely.*

Going back to school was going to be a full-time gig. It had to be. In addition to attending an average of twenty hours of class each week, I needed to study another twenty hours. If that wasn't enough, I would be squeezing in another fifteen hours to practice what I would be learning by driving my portable massage table to the homes of friends, family, and friends of friends.

If you've been keeping up with the math, that's about 55 hours each week, not including travel time. Debbie would have her hands full taking care of our young daughter while I was in school, and I wouldn't have time for a job. My parents offered us the opportunity to live in their 1,500-square-foot basement so we could save money and Debbie could have my mother's help with our young daughter Ashley. We couldn't pass it up. Now that we we'd be living 65 miles south of the massage school in Seattle not having to pay rent made the expense of frequent trips to the gas station a little easier to handle. We moved back to Olympia in the summer of 1990 and set up our temporary home in my parents' basement.

My assumptions about the education I would receive at Brian's school proved true. Twelve months after beginning school, I graduated. Two months later, I received my professional license from the Washington State Board of Health. Two weeks after that, Debbie and I welcomed our second daughter, Sara. Heavy with a sense of family responsibility, I began my new career at a large health club, where I quickly proved to myself that, indeed, I *could* use my hands to help people with soft-tissue injuries.

I knew I had made the right career choice—but I had the wrong job. Instead of helping people cope with injury-related pain, I was mostly giving simple relaxation massage, and, disappointingly, it was feeling increasingly monotonous. I had been there only two years, but once again, I was ready for a change.

Having decided to shift away from a health club environment, and knowing I possessed an entrepreneurial spirit, I took yet another risk and decided to build my own medical massage practice. I rented a small clinic space in a medical park which I shared with an osteopathic sports physician and a gastroenterologist.

Now I was where I wanted to be.

Much to the delight of my wife and parents, my determination paid off and my appointment calendar started to fill up. At first, people scheduled appointments with me because their regular therapist didn't have any openings available. This seemed to become an issue for a number of therapists in our area because after receiving their first deep tissue massage from me, most continued to see *me*. I wasn't exactly stealing clients from any of my competition, but I was providing something different from what my clients had previously experienced. It was a blend of techniques I had learned and then modified, along with other treatment techniques I had developed myself through trial and error.

In truth, I do not like using the word *massage* to describe my profession. In part, it's because of how massage has been viewed by the average American, especially back in the early nineties. Most people saw massage as something sensual or perverse, more so if their first experience of receiving massage was in Bangkok, Thailand, or if they watched the episode of

Seinfeld when George Costanza was *stuck* receiving his massage from—a *dude.* It was especially true if the person's first thoughts conjured visions of masseuses giving rubdowns in skanky massage parlors.

I'm not a *masseuse.* Technically, that would require a gender reassignment surgery and hormone therapies since that is the French word for *female* massage therapists. Please don't call me a *masseur* either. Although that's the correct French word for a male massage therapist, it still sounds a bit shady. Technically, I am a *licensed massage therapist,* but the more accurate label for what I do is that of a *medical myotherapist.* Simply put, myotherapy involves treating the structures of the body, including the muscles and other soft tissues, with the purpose of decreasing dysfunction and pain while increasing function and mobility.

From the start, my work was different, and my clients and patients were healing from their injuries after just a few treatments. When local physicians heard about my patients experiencing rapid recovery from my myotherapy techniques, the referrals began flowing in, and my schedule was full.

Within two years of launching my business, I had hired over a half-dozen therapists to handle the number of people wanting to be seen. On a regular basis, I trained my therapists to duplicate the techniques I had been perfecting, and as their skills increased, so did our client volume. Eventually, we had grown so much we needed to move into a larger clinic space in an adjacent medical office.

The years passed, and I continued to add therapists to our treatment staff, making sure to dedicate enough time each week to teaching them the unique medical massage techniques I had been perfecting. As much as I enjoyed training the therapists, though, I also wished I did not have to *re*-train every therapist I hired.

If only there were a school that prepared their graduates to perform medical myotherapy and other related massage techniques rather than requiring them to need additional training after graduating.

My idea of launching a medically-based massage school took root, and the planning began. If you are an entrepreneur yourself, you can no doubt relate when I describe the flurry of creative ideas that constantly flooded my consciousness. Mainly swirling around my head were visions of opening the country's first medically-based massage and myotherapy school and what its healing potential could be. I very much wanted to develop something unique to our profession— something different that would stand out amongst the hundreds of massage schools already in existence across the country. So, notebook in hand, I would write down every idea which came to mind, day or night. Often the ideas flowed most freely just as I was drifting off to sleep, forcing me to grab my glasses, turn on the light, and scribble down my ideas before they evaporated into the night.

I told everyone who would listen about my dream of my own massage school. My vision became more and more clear with every friend, family member, or colleague I shared it with. Then, at some point, I knew it was no longer just a dream. It was happening!

I felt strongly that my new school should be located in a hospital. There were—and still are—two hospitals in our county. One of them, Providence St. Peter Hospital, is a non-profit Catholic hospital. My efforts to locate my school there were short-lived, as the school was a for-profit business, and there would be issues with their nonprofit status. That left me with just one option: the for-profit hospital adjacent to where my clinic was located at the time.

Capital Medical Center had gone through difficult times when they first opened in 1985 as the Black Hills Community Hospital. Community members, who had faithfully contributed philanthropic gifts to the nonprofit St. Pete's, held a negative community view of a for-profit hospital. It took years for that to fade, but as the quality of services grew and increasing numbers of respected physicians applied for admitting privileges there, the hospital eventually earned the high regard it deserved. When a beautiful new 65,000 square foot, four-story addition was built onto the south side of the hospital in 1995, the hospital's reputation was further elevated. All but half of the top floor of the addition, called the Physicians Pavilion, was made into office and clinical space to support the doctors working there.

It was four years later when I began looking for space for our new massage school. When I learned that the unused half of the fourth floor still remained vacant, I was certain our school belonged there.

Unfortunately, those with the power to make that happen were flatly against the idea.

"It's called a 'Physicians Pavilion' for a reason, Bob," they said. Besides the fact I wasn't a *physician*, the majority of the decision-makers considered "medical massage" to be an oxy-moron. At that time, if a doctor did prescribe massage for a patient, it was more likely with an "it can't hurt" philosophy as opposed to the physician's actual belief in its healing efficacy.

So I reluctantly accepted their refusals and found a small commercial space just down the street from the hospital. Although I knew in my heart that the school belonged *inside* Capital Medical Center, I went ahead and negotiated a fifteen-month lease on my new space.

"Why only fifteen months?" asked Shelly, the leasing agent. I confidently replied, "That gives us three months to advertise the school, give tours, and register our first class, and another twelve months to graduate that first class from the program. I believe we will be moving the school into Capital Medical Center by the end of this lease." I smiled as I signed the lease and handed her a check.

This is temporary, I kept repeating to myself. *Fifteen months of lease payments, and that will be it. We are meant to be in the hospital. There is no plan B.*

Shortly after I launched the initial advertising campaign, I remember my father asking me one day, rather bluntly, "So, Bobby, what happens if this doesn't work out?"

I mirrored back my father's grim expression and replied, "We lose everything."

"Everything?"

"Everything," I said, nodding affirmatively.

"I couldn't do that", he said, shaking his head. "You've got a lot of guts."

In the first three months of our lease, we were able to fill the class with twenty-two cash-paying students, and we taught our first class in the spring of 2000. I remember being overwhelmed with excitement as I watched my dreams come into fruition. It was indeed a promising beginning. We weren't where we wanted to be, but it was a great start.

During a staff meeting in early summer, my mobile phone began to ring. I apologized to my staff for forgetting to silence my phone, and as I was about to turn it off, I could see that the call was coming from Capital Medical Center.

"I'm sorry, but I have to take this call," I sheepishly said to the teachers as their looks revealed various degrees of irritation.

"This is Bob…" I answered.

"Bob? Bob Haase? The massage therapist?" asked the voice on the other end.

"Yes, speaking. How can I help you?"

"Uh, Mr. Haase, this is Jana St. James at the emergency room here at Capital Medical Center, We have a 55-year-old male patient here who was brought in by ambulance with excruciating back pain. He is a patrol officer for the Washington State Patrol and has a condition that precludes us from administering any type of anti-inflammatory or pain medication. He says you worked on him several years ago and were the only one who could help. We've never really been in this situation before, but would you be willing to come over here as soon as possible?"

My heart raced. I smiled broadly and said, "Yes! I'll be there in less than five minutes!" I ended the call and looked at my staff. Still smiling, I said, "So … I need to go. Someone at the hospital needs my help, and it cannot wait."

Less than five minutes later I arrived at the emergency reception desk and was immediately escorted back past the triage area and into the officer's curtained cubicle. Although it had been several years, I immediately recognized Trooper Preston Beegle from the treatments I had given him. Preston tried to stop his howling and moaning, but he could barely speak. Tears rolled down his cheeks as he writhed, trying to find a position that would relieve his pain. Two trauma team doctors, two nurses, and an anesthesiologist were gathered around the gurney with looks of confusion on their faces.

"You, uh, you are a 'massage therapist,' Mr. Haase? Is that right?" asked one of the doctors.

"I am. I am licensed as a 'massage therapist,' but I specialize in the practice of myotherapy and related medical massage techniques." Then I turned back to focus my attention on the patient.

"Preston, it looks like you are in incredible pain. Can you tell me what's going on?" I asked him. He could not. "Preston, I want you to nod to my 'yes' or 'no' questions, okay?" He nodded in the affirmative.

"Preston, is it the low back? The same pain I treated you for a few years ago?" Indeed it was. A few more yes/no questions later, I instructed the staff who were observing to help maneuver him for me. "Don't leave... I'm going to have you help me move him twice more before I'm done. The entire treatment will take less than five minutes." Their brows furrowed a bit, confused about how I was going to help in such a short time.

I began treating Preston with the low back release work I had been teaching my staff therapists over the years. As I worked, his pain increased. The medical staff looked concerned, but Preston and I knew his discomfort would be fleeting. Within a few minutes, his breathing slowed as breaths became deeper and more purposed. His moaning subsided, and his tears stopped. When I finished and took my hands off of his injured muscles, he let out a deep sigh. The pain was gone. With a relaxed voice confirming his relief, Preston smiled and said, "Thank you, Bob. Thank you so much. The pain is 100 percent gone."

I will never forget the faces of the trauma team members when I looked back at them. All five of them literally had their mouths hanging open, unable to understand what just happened. They stood silent until they seemed to be waking up from some sort of dream-state.

"What did you just do?" the lead E.R. doctor asked me.

"It's simple. Officer Beegle here sits in his car most of the day, shortening his iliopsoas muscles. When he gets out of his car, the shortened muscles put excessive force on his quadratus lumborum muscles in his low back, which are trying to help him stand up erect. The QLs are weaker, so they get abused by the antagonists, the psoas group, and I have to 'break up the fight,' so to speak. I simply applied a version of strain/counterstrain and proprioceptive neuromuscular facilitation to release the tension. If he remembers to stretch his legs more often during his shifts, he won't need a follow-up treatment. Simple stuff. I teach this to every student in my school in our treatment protocols."

It was less than a week later that I received a call from Capital Medical Center's property management office. It was Miriam Forrest, the agent responsible for leasing all of the hospital's private office and clinic space. "How many square feet do you need for your school?" Miriam asked me.

Within two weeks, we had negotiated a five-year lease for half of the fourth-floor space in the hospital's Physicians Pavilion.

My energy and enthusiasm for the school's potential increased and I became even more engrossed in my work. Ultimately, my marriage began to suffer as I spent more and more time away from home. Working ninety hours a week to provide for my family eventually morphed into working ninety hours a week to pay child support and spousal maintenance. (As I would realize some time later, my own actions had led to my own adversity. But more on that later.

I don't mean to sound like a fatalist, but there is a sad irony in working excessively to provide for a family that you will eventually lose because of your work. I have come to realize that, except for providing for the basic needs of your family, like food and shelter, your job will never be as important as your family. When your loved ones start feeling that your work is more important than everything else in your life, especially them, the consequences can be dire. You don't have to lose your family because your priorities have spun out of balance. Live more simply, suppress your desire to "have it all" to impress others, take the time to build relationships with those you love. If work is your priority, you may arrive home from work one day only to realize you've lost what is most important to you.

I learned that lesson too late.

About a year after my divorce from Debbie was final, I began to feel pain under the left side of my tongue. The doctors assured me it wasn't cancer. "Maybe Leukoplakia?" was the unofficial diagnosis. Although *maybe* isn't a diagnosis, it was enough of an answer to satisfy me at the time.

Meanwhile, I had married my daughter's riding instructor, Jennifer—someone I would never have been in a relationship with had I been thinking clearly. While she met some of my needs, we were cut from a different cloth, and our relationship increasingly drew out my worst qualities. Jennifer was fourteen years my junior and we had nothing in common. It was good to feel wanted by someone, but was she right for me? No. After three tumultuous years of marriage, Jennifer and I separated and divorced.

The end of my second marriage caused me to ponder marrying my children's mother at the wise old age of twenty-three. Looking back, I have come to understand that I didn't truly grasp what it was I was getting myself into or what marriage would require of me. I was selfish, ambitious, and immature. I didn't understand what a *covenant-based* relationship was, which is loving another as a *choice* rather than because of how she makes me feel.

In the years since I have learned that the marriage covenant is not a *transaction*, but a decision to love 'til *death do us part*. I never took the time to build a foundation or strengthen that marriage. In fact, I never truly entered the marriage as I should have, allowing my roots to intertwine with hers so we could grow stronger in our bond and more connected over time. When I finally did learn, the relationship was long over.

But the consequences of a broken family live on. The adversity my family and I experienced from that divorce hasn't so much happened *to* me, but *because of* me. I know now that, ultimately, my marriage ended because of my inactions as well as my actions.

Meanwhile, the pain under my tongue continued to worsen ...

CHAPTER TWO
Not Mine to Have

I remember sitting in my office, alone, when my doctor called to give me the news. It was a September morning in 2008—two years since I had first sensed pain under my tongue.

Dr. Myers cut right to it: "Bob, you have cancer."

Before we go on, let me be clear: I never *had* cancer because the cancer was never mine to claim. Cancer is a cruel and insidious assault by a person's own body attempting to commit suicide. It is physiological mutiny. I had cancer, but the cancer was *not mine to have.*

As he delivered the diagnosis, Dr. Myers' voice was calm yet laden with angst. He did his best to sound positive as he spoke the troubling words. Although what he said had brought a numbing punch, I was strangely relieved. I had been experiencing constant pain for two years and the doctors had not understood *why*.

My very first biopsy had been done two years earlier. As discomfort had turned to pain and the pain had gotten worse, my family doctor had referred me to Dr. Carl Myers, Group Health Cooperative's lead otolaryngologist, more commonly known as an ENT, or ear, nose, and throat specialist.

After checking in, I was taken into Dr. Myers's procedure room where I spent a few minutes with his nurse for the usual "pre-visit interrogation." She reviewed my current medications, checked my blood pressure, and asked about my worsening symptoms.

Dr. Myers eventually knocked on the exam room door and entered. He had a warm smile which put me immediately at ease. He made small talk, asked about my family, and wanted to know where my latest travels had taken me. He had gentle, caring facial expressions and tone of voice—the kind of bedside manner which would make any nervous patient feel safe in a doctor's office.

For a better understanding of what was taking place in my mouth and throat, Dr. Myers said he'd need to take a closer look. He apologized as he gently placed a thin straw connected to a small aerosol canister into each of my nostrils and applied a quick spritz of a hideous-smelling substance—a combination of Lidocaine to numb me and Afrin to decongest. After a minute or so, he took his special diagnostic hose with a tiny camera and light attached and began snaking it down one of my nostrils until it descended nearly a foot down my throat. Even though my throat was numb, I could still feel that tube dangling in places where it shouldn't have been. I suppose it's a blessing

I don't have much of a gag reflex.

At that point, Dr. Myers became my personal *otorhino-laryngological tour guide* of sorts, describing what he saw as he looked around in the dark cavity. He gradually maneuvered the flexible camera-hose (endoscope) down my trachea, descending even deeper to inspect the tissues as he looked for signs of disease. When he had seen enough, he slowly and gently pulled the tube up and out. My body shuddered as the last length of hose finally made its exit and slid over the paper towel in his hand. Ugh. It felt like a mechanic pulling the oil stick from a car's engine to see if it was a quart low or not.

Next, wooden tongue depressor in hand, Dr. Myers tilted down the microscope apparatus, which was mounted to the halo-strap wrapped around his head, and began his search for irregular tissues. After locating the suspicious cells where I had been experiencing pain, he scheduled a hospital visit to remove the abnormal tissues from my tongue.

That first biopsy turned out to be more of a surgical procedure with general anesthesia, my family gathered in the waiting room, and me wearing a blue cotton gown, which wasn't designed to cover a bare bottom as well as one would hope. After waking up in a state of delirium, I was sent home to rest my tongue, which was being held together with several sutures.

Two days later, Dr. Myers called me with the pathology results. With genuine relief in his voice, he announced, "Good news, Robert! It's not cancer." I was happy with the news, but at the same time, being told *what it wasn't* was not the explanation I was looking for. However, it did put an end to the pain, albeit only temporarily.

Six months later, I began to feel the same pain I had experienced initially, in the very same spot. Frustrated, I returned for another session with Dr. Myers. Again, it was confirmed that he needed to perform another biopsy to cut out the suspicious white cells, which were causing the pain on the underside surface of my tongue.

For the record, I absolutely despise surgeries. I hate voluntarily giving up my consciousness, as I confess to being a bit of a control freak, but I'm working on that. Resolved to avoid another visit to the operating room In the hospital, I asked Dr. Myers if he could perform the biopsy in his own procedure room. Thankfully he obliged, against his better judgment. His staff was a bit dumbfounded at the very thought.

Shortly after I arrived at his clinic and checked in, his medical assistant once again took my blood pressure, asked the usual health history questions, and then handed me a clipboard containing numerous medical releases. The forms were full of common medical language such as, "Your procedure could result in unintended outcomes, like death." After reading the death warning, I grinned, skipped to the bottom, and signed my name. I wasn't worried. It was not my day to die.

Dr. Myers and his nurse, Dixie, entered the procedure room and explained to me what would be taking place. The doctor appeared a little uneasy, likely because he was swimming into somewhat uncharted waters. As I was about to find out, this was the first time his patient would be awake during a procedure requiring him to excise such a large amount of tissue.

The doctor stood by my side, holding a syringe with a long, large-bore needle. It looked more menacing than anything my dentists had ever used on me. Just before injecting me with Lidocaine mixed with Epinephrine to constrict the blood vessels and help reduce the bleeding, he took a deep breath, then exhaled.

"Ready?" he asked me.

"Yep. Go ahead," I answered apprehensively. Delaying the inevitable was not an option.

The nurse reached out and took my hand, holding it firmly. At first, I thought it was a nice gesture but not really necessary until the doctor drove the large-bore needle deep into my tongue. Wow! This was a whole different kind of pain. My entire body stiffened, and I stopped breathing for several seconds. Finally, I exhaled and leaned back into the reclined procedure chair, allowing my body to relax.

After several deep injections, my tongue was sufficiently numb. With a square of gauze, the nurse securely pulled and held my tongue to expose the suspicious tissue for the doctor's scalpel. The paper bib that hung from my neck shielded my shirt from the flying droplets of blood, catching most of it, but not all.

As the nurse held my tongue with one hand, she tried reaching with her other to assist the doctor by handing him implements and gauze as needed. I could see that look in her eyes which said, "I need more hands!" As I had been instructed, I held my hand up to signal to the doctor that I wanted to say something.

"My hands work fine," I said, my mouth filled with cotton balls and my tongue growing increasingly numb. "Let me have some gauze and I can hold my tongue out of the way so Dixie can be more helpful. I won't even ask for a discount." I chuckle now at how ridiculous I must have sounded.

The kind doctor paused, nodded approval, and replied, "If you're sure, we can try it." Dixie handed me a fresh square of gauze.

Once he was sure my tongue was completely numb, and with a scalpel in one hand and tweezers in the other, Dr. Myers began slicing away, scooping out the suspicious tissue as well as some of the adjacent healthy tissue. Leaving a "V-channel" that would be easier to close, he and the nurse worked quickly, sopping up the blood and applying silver nitrate to cauterize the tissues before suturing my tongue back together.

To this day, Dr. Myers tells me I remain his only patient to assist in their own procedure.

For two years, that same scenario was repeated over and over again. I tried keeping a confident attitude, but my frustration was building as the recurring pain never seemed to go away for long, resulting in biopsy after biopsy, and the doctor calling each time to repeat the same "good news."

When I received my next "Good news, it's not cancer!" phone call, my affable attitude suddenly faded. Exasperated, I said, "You know, Doc, I'm also not pregnant. I've been spending a lot of time and money to find out what I don't have. Let's get a pathologist on this who can give us an answer as to what I do have."

So that September, Dr. Myers performed a significant biopsy, taking a broader and deeper swath of tissue than he had in the past. Then he sent samples to several labs across the country hoping one of them would figure the whole thing out.

Ultimately, it was the Albert Einstein College of Medicine in New York City that solved the mystery.

"We were able to identify the anomaly in the tissue sample," the Albert Einstein lab pathologist told Dr. Myers. "Your patient has squamous cell carcinoma."

Upon hearing the news, I felt relieved in a way. Finally, I had an explanation for the pain I had been experiencing for the past two years. I couldn't make sense of it. I wasn't a smoker. Didn't chew tobacco. Didn't have Human Papillmavirus (HPV).

It just was what it was.

I had drawn the *C-card.*

Following each procedure, I would return home for the recovery phase, which was almost always the same: I would watch the clock and wait for the intense pain to emerge as the local anesthetic began to wear off. Pain meds certainly helped, but since the tongue is such a highly sensitive body part, I found only minimal relief. It was the ice water I continually rinsed my mouth with which gave me the most relief. (If my parents ask, it was the thick and creamy, 32 ounce, 1500-calorie hot fudge malted milkshakes they brought me from Baskin-Robbins.)

My early interactions with Dr. Myers and his medical staff were pleasant enough, but after numerous visits, they all started to feel like family. With each visit, the banter evolved from typical small talk to more personal topics, such as the ongoing saga of my personal life—whom I had been dating, where I had traveled, how my seminars were going, and the like. As I think back on those days, those personal connections I made there in Dr. Myers' office, mixed with plenty of humor, made each daunting process easier to endure. I'll never forget how we all howled one time after I arrived at the office, hopped up onto the now-familiar procedure chair, and deadpanned, "Hey, Doc. Just a little off the sides, please."

After each excision, to ensure the doctor got it all, the lab pathologist would study the tissue cut from my tongue, but the results would always be the same. Dr. Myers would call a day or so later to say, "Good news, you're cancer-free!"

The cancer, with a narcissistic personality all its own, was never truly satisfied that I was repeatedly losing tiny pieces of my tongue. Every six to twelve months, the pain would return to the same spot on the underside of my tongue, which would then be biopsied, only for me to—once again— be declared, "cancer-free." I felt like I was starring in my own "Groundhog Day," reliving the same scenario over and over.

CHAPTER THREE
With a Vengeance

Meanwhile, the economy was in a state of turmoil and faltering; that time is now commonly referred to as the *Great Recession.* The vocational school I had built from scratch into the nation's only hospital-based school of its kind had to close its doors.

Most of our students had been covering their tuition expenses with student loans funded by Sallie Mae, with 85 percent approval rates. But the approval rates began dropping precipitously. Within weeks, every student loan application for our upcoming licensing program was rejected.

The hard costs of keeping our doors open—more than $50,000 a month—drained our reserves quickly. We had to do something, and we had to do it soon. Hesitation would have been catastrophic.

We kept our concerns to the confines of my office. I instructed our upper management staff not to tell the students about the potential collapse of our school. There was no reason to distress the students or create an atmosphere of worry and insecurity. We had a duty to our current students; we had promised them an incredible education that would make each of them exceptional massage therapists when they completed our program, and we still intended to do that.

But I also knew that if we didn't have enough students enrolled in our upcoming classes who actually had the cash to pay the $10,000+ course costs, we would have to refund all of the monies paid to us by applicants thus far and close the school. The good news is that we were able to get all of our students graduated, but the bad news was our failure to get enough cash-paying students registered before the course start date. We were forced to shut down the school. Over 300 massage schools closed that year for the same reason. The heaviness on my heart was overwhelming.

We rented a small venue and threw ourselves a heckuva farewell party. But when the party ended, I had a hard truth to face: I was ruined financially, and I wasn't sure what I was going to do about it.

So, to recap: First, my marriage fell apart. Then, I was diagnosed with cancer. Then I had to close my business and lay off my employees during a horrible economy. As the sole stockholder in the school cosigning for each of our company leases and loans, I lost my house and watched as my BMW was towed away by the "repo man." Crashing wave after crashing wave of unimaginable adversity seemed determined to knock me down before I even had a chance to regain my footing and pre-pare for the next wave. The last straw was a painful kidney stone that sent me to the emergency room the week after my divorce was finalized. That thirteen-month period left me more bruised and battered than I want to think about.

In the years that followed, I began building a small contin-uing education company, presenting my course, Secrets of Deep Tissue™, for licensed massage therapists and chiroprac-tors. Unfortunately, while I was diligently working to build my seminar business, the cancer seemed to never truly go away.

By the time five years had passed, I had already undergone a total of eleven surgical procedures and biopsies on my tongue. The pain had returned, but it was more severe and looked different.

Dr. Myers, still my ENT, scheduled me for another surgery in which he was only able to remove half of the tumor. He in-formed me after the procedure that the tumor had grown, and I was going to need more surgery, but someone even more qualified would be required to do it.

By good fortune, it turned out that the best surgeon in the country for the type of cancer I had was on staff at Virginia Ma-son Hospital in Seattle, just an hour north of my home. Due to the urgency of my case, I was able to get an appointment just a few days later.

The following week I drove to Virginia Mason for a consul-tation with Dr. Stephen Bayles, who explained to me in detail what needed to be done. It was pretty much the same thing I had heard before, but this time would be riskier, and a larger portion of tissue would have to be removed. Dr. Bayles explained to me that there was a real possibility I would not be able to speak again after the surgery.

The idea that I might never speak the same way again started to become real and ominous. I tried to project strength amidst the news of my future changing. I knew I needed to maintain focus.

"We will meet again after your surgery to discuss what treatment will be most appropriate going forward," Dr. Bayles said, but the tears had already started flowing. Trying to comprehend what would lie ahead of me was nearly impossible. It felt huge, and vast, and insurmountable. From somewhere in the back of my head, I heard a weak but determined voice repeating, *This will NOT slow me down ... This will NOT slow me down ....*

"I was only able to get half," Dr. Bayles said after the surgery, with a soft voice that revealed his frustration.

What!? Are you kidding me?? My mind was racing. Was I experiencing déjà vu? Those were the same words Dr. Myers had said to me, not even a month earlier.

Dr. Bayles went on to explain the cancer was extremely aggressive and had grown faster than he had expected. It was moving quickly, and time was not on my side. He wanted to wait to see what the pathology report revealed, but he already knew he needed to go back in and perform yet another surgery, and soon.

"This time, Robert, I'll need to remove even more tissue in order to get it all," Dr. Bayles said. "If the pathology report comes back as I believe it will, we will need to take out the entire left half of your tongue."

He went on to assure me I would eventually regain my ability to speak, assuming the nerves that supported speech weren't damaged during surgery.

"You will have difficulty speaking at first, but eventually, you should be able to communicate."

My heart sank.

I was a public speaker. I had to be able to talk! How would I earn a living? I needed my tongue! I remember how, as I was trying to digest and comprehend what the doctor was telling me, I became light-headed, almost ready to pass out. It was all too surreal. I had always been a glass-half-full type of person who could see the good in everything. I had always believed in God and that He had a plan for my life. *But now this? How could this be part of His plan?*

I was waiting the next day for word on the pathology report when Dr. Bayles came into my hospital room. His face instantly told me that what he was about to say wouldn't be good.

"The pathologist has thoroughly evaluated the tissue I removed yesterday morning," he said. "As I mentioned to you in the recovery room, the cancer has very aggressive features. I'm sorry to tell you the report isn't what I had hoped."

Those are words no one ever wants to hear. After all these years, the worst-case scenario had finally come to fruition.

Dr. Bayles told me that he had scheduled a surgery suite for three days later.

Lastly, he added, "Due to the spread of the cancer outside of your mouth and into your lymph nodes, you are going to need not just radiation, but chemotherapy as well, beginning a few weeks after you return home." He was doing his best to be reassuring, which wasn't an easy task given the magnitude of his news.

"Can I wait a few months to tie up some loose ends and *then* have the surgery?" I asked, optimistically.

"No," he replied gently. "This can't wait."

I was emotionally numb. I was trying to take in all of what Dr. Bayles was telling me, but his words were unimaginable. My life was on the line, and I didn't have the luxury of time. I felt I was dreaming—or in someone else's nightmare. *This wasn't in my script! What will my life be like with half of a tongue? How can I support myself if I can't talk? What will people think of me with a speech impediment? Was this really God's plan for my life???* The inevitable reality was starting to become clear: If I did not let the surgeon do what he needed to do, I could likely be gone in a matter of months.

CHAPTER FOUR
Treatment–A Deadly Cure

The surgery went exactly as planned. In the post-surgery recovery area, even though I was still drowsy in my post-anesthesia fog, I could see the tears streaming down my three daughters' faces as they took turns gently holding my hands in theirs. They didn't have to utter a word because their faces reaffirmed that I was blessed with children who love me. Unconditional love from anyone is huge, but when your children give you that gift, no matter what situation you are in, it makes all the difference.

Even though those next few days are a blur, I'll never forget the kindness and graciousness with which the nurses attended to me. As you can imagine, a post-surgical patient doesn't always look his best, and the scene isn't always very pretty. Still, the nurses did whatever they could to keep me clean and make me as comfortable as possible. I realized that what I was experiencing had an upside: I was seeing how people can demonstrate genuine empathy toward others despite their unappealing outward appearance. I was now on the receiving end of that kind of compassion, and I was learning how important and impactful the gift of unconditional love and acceptance can be.

While I was having a particularly difficult time one night, the night shift nurse could hear me moaning from extreme discomfort, so she came into my room to check on me. Seeing I was in distress, she sat on the edge of my bed and began speaking to me in calming, gentle tones with a warm and comforting smile. She explained what was happening in my mouth and how my body was responding was normal. Her words were purposeful, helping me gain perspective while at the same time distracting me from my fears and discomfort. She spent nearly an hour with me, holding my hand and sharing some of her life experiences, all intended to shift my focus and, in effect, talk me down off the emotional cliff I was clinging to

As I carefully typed my responses to her stories on my laptop, I realized I had stopped focusing on my own situation and had started giving her words of encouragement about *her* being a wife and mother. It was amazing how my intense pain from just moments earlier began to subside as we took the focus off of *me.*

It had been five days since my surgery, and I still didn't have the results back from the pathologist to verify there were safe margins on the tissues that had been removed. I was beyond frustrated. And then Dr. Bayles came into my room.

Suddenly, all my stress, all my pain, and all my emotions took a brief pause as I heard my surgeon say the words, "Bob, we got it all." *Praise God.* The cancer had been removed, and clear margins were confirmed! I felt as though my *thankfulness meter* had been reset. Thanks to Dr. Bayles and the prayers of so many of my supporters, I was—at long last—cancer-free!

My elation was tempered, of course, knowing I had been told the same thing several times before. On one hand, I was thanking God for the news I had waited so long to hear, but my intellect was also reminding me: *Don't get too excited. If you've learned anything from this experience, it is that anything can happen.* As Dr. Cobbie Whitten, a psychologist specializing in oncology, later told me, "You may be cancer-free, but you will never be free of cancer."

Later that week, I woke up from an afternoon nap thinking about my friends and family members and all their *life stuff.* I knew some of them had been dealing with significant issues of their own, but still, they didn't want to bother and burden me with their troubles because they believed my situation was worse than theirs.

Over those twelve days in the hospital, and in the weeks following, I encouraged a couple of friends to tell me about the challenges they were facing. Just like the night a caring nurse had sat on my bed sharing quiet conversation, I found that hearing about my friends' problems allowed me to redirect my attention outwardly rather than remain fixated on my own situation. I welcomed the distractions. From that, I came to understand a simple truth: Pain is pain, and our perception of pain is individually relative for each of us. More so, our *pain threshold* adapts to our current situation and makes our hearts hurt just the same.

While a patient at Virginia Mason Hospital, I knew how blessed I was to have Dr. Bayles as my surgeon. To this day, he is considered one of the best in the country for his skills and surgical techniques that are so unique, his work can be identified by merely looking at it! One afternoon, Dr. Bayles told me about how he and his 15-year-old son had seen my story covered on the evening news. His son had been extremely impressed with the surgery and its outcomes.

"That was awesome!" he said to his dad. "Whoever figured out how to do that must be really smart!"

"Uh, that was me," the proud father replied. "I did that."

Let's think about that for a moment. What a powerful moment that was in that boy's life, realizing his father was so smart that he could save a patient's life with the creative and expert use of a scalpel, needle, and thread. That moment will be burned into his son's memory, likely encouraging him to make his own mark on the world one day.

Life is full of pivotal moments. Mine was the moment I heard the words, "We need to remove the left half of your tongue if you want to live." I know now that while I may have experienced loss, I didn't lose what was important. Not only that, but there was something wonderful happening, leading me in a different direction on a new course for the better.

When I was finally discharged from the hospital, a friend drove me home to Olympia. As we pulled into the driveway, I was overwhelmed, realizing I was finally back home and so incredibly blessed by those who had been selflessly supporting me.

This whole cancer experience had brought change and healing not only into my own heart but also into the hearts of people who cared about me. What I had been through helped to make them increasingly aware that life is far too short to take people for granted. It also led to the strengthening of many relationships in ways I could never have foreseen.

Whenever I would start worrying about my future, I would take inventory of the blessings I had in my life. Simple things. I concentrated and began to list them one by one. I had three amazing daughters who loved me unconditionally. I had incredible parents who dropped everything to be by my side for those twelve days in the hospital. I had good friends who had not abandoned me. And most important, I still had my life and all the unknown opportunities it presented. As the list grew, my anxiousness about what my future was going to look like was slowly replaced by a sense of calm, and my fear replaced with gratefulness and peace.

Several days after my return home, I began editing video footage from a lecture I had given about a month before my surgery. The footage was going to be shown in seminars led by my teaching staff while I was home recuperating. Sitting at my computer trimming the individual video clips, I couldn't help but notice how rich and strong my voice had sounded then. As each clip played and I heard my former self at the top of my game, a deep sadness came over me.

At one time, I had taken pride in the depth of tone and ra-dio-quality of my speaking voice. I had taken for granted that it would always be there for my use. Now, I knew I would never again sound as I did on the video recordings. That voice was gone. Sure, I would recover to some degree and work diligently to speak and be understood, yet I knew that that confident, fa-miliar voice would never sound the same again.

Leaning forward in my chair, my hands holding my face, the tears started forming in the corners of my eyes. All of a sud-den, I was overwhelmed by what I had lost. From this point on, I'd be speaking with an imperfect voice which would require an audience to have to pay full attention and listen carefully if they had any hope in understanding me. It was a bitter pill to swal-low that day.

Luckily, I was reminded of the encouraging words of a dear friend who had once said to me, "It is not about your voice, Bob. It's about the message."

One morning the week before my chemo and radiation were scheduled to start, I was in my kitchen standing by the sink. As I looked down at the rubber feeding tube hanging from my belly and fumbled with the tube adapter, I thought about the dramatic transformations of my face and mouth. Every morning when I looked in the mirror, my face looked like Mr. Potato Head[2], with transient swelling, which seemed to re-shape it daily. *How could I ever go out in public again?*

My youngest daughter, Holly, is incredibly empathetic. It wasn't difficult for her to pick up on the emotions I was holding inside when she found me in the kitchen. I had been going

---

[2] Mr. Potato Head®, Hasbro, Inc.

through various scenarios in my imagination: *What if I succumbed to cancer and couldn't be there for my daughters?* I tried to focus and be positive, but I wasn't able to hold it together.

Holly wrapped her arms around me for a long, warm embrace. I was quivering—not breathing for fear of losing control. I tried to hold back the tears, to be strong so as not to frighten Holly, but I failed and began to weep uncontrollably. As I leaned over the kitchen counter with my face buried in my hands, Holly held me and cried with me.

It felt like our roles had reversed, and I wasn't sure that it was fair to Holly. I was the father. I was supposed to be the example of strength. Not the other way around. It was far more of a mental war than I had expected it would be, and the awfulness of chemotherapy and radiation had not even started yet.

It was now two weeks since my surgery, and my parents drove me to my appointment with the radiation oncologist. As Dr. Vera entered my examination room, her face drew an apologetic smile as she reached out her arms and pulled me in for a hug. I smiled as this tiny red-headed woman, who was now six months into her pregnancy, got up on her toes to hug me. More doctors should do that.

In conjunction with my radiation treatments, I was also going to have chemotherapy. Enter Dr. Xingwei Sui of Group Health Cooperative's oncology department. Dr. Sui is an exceptional doctor who is quick to offer a big smile and a two-handed handshake. When he entered my room for the first time, he greeted me and put his hand on my shoulder. With a warm, assuring smile and a thick Chinese accent, he said, "Robert, I am going to take care of you. It will not be easy, but I am going to help you through this." There was something about his gentle spirit that both comforted me and gave me hope.

The connections each member of my medical team made with me had an immeasurable impact on my healing. Their words of encouragement weren't full of empty promises, because every one of my doctors thoroughly explained the potential adverse outcomes from their treatment. Their sincerity and caring helped give me confidence that I would survive as well as the sense I would live a fuller and more purposeful life because of my experiences.

It should be the norm, but it isn't always that way.

In the mid-nineties, years before my issues with cancer, I was invited to be on a panel of alternative healthcare providers speaking to a room filled with physicians who were finishing their residencies. The panel also included a naturopath, an acupuncturist, a chiropractor, a Reiki energy practitioner, an aromatherapist, and a foot reflexologist.

The moderator of the panel asked us each to answer how we would treat a patient with a specific ailment. One by one, each of the practitioners explained their individual specialty, how it is performed, and why it is effective. When it was my turn to answer, I simply reminded them, "I think if we would all just start by hugging our patients, I bet half would begin to improve just from knowing someone cares. The simple act of reaching out and putting your hand on a shoulder or arm as you talk has incredibly positive effects on the human body[3]."

---

[3] Kory, Floyd (2014) Relational and Health Correlates of Affection Deprivation. Western Journal of Communication, 78:4, 383-403,

On the first day of my chemo/radiation treatment, I learned that I was scheduled for five treatments a week for six weeks. I couldn't help but notice the possible side effects of the treatment that were listed on the release form I had to sign. Severe nausea and vomiting. Diarrhea. Temporary hair loss. Inability to smell or taste food. Damage to my veins and other vital organs. Research also told me about possible permanent effects on the clarity of my thoughts and memory changes, which all were eventually proven true by the end of my treatment.

While the negative possibilities were grim, there was also a huge upside: This chemo/radiation treatment would give me the best chance possible to survive the aggressiveness of the cancer and see all three of my daughters grow into the women they were destined to become. It also would allow me to live each day with my family nearby, to contribute to the community and world I live in, to be able to travel, and make many more of my dreams become reality. The treatments would be giving me the option of a future.

As we entered the treatment room for the first time, I felt oddly comforted seeing the dozens of molded mesh masks hanging along the wall. Each one with a patient's name written on it in permanent marker. There were so many masks, each in the shape of a stranger's face, each containing a different story—a story of a life interrupted. Stories of lives impacted, and futures forever changed. Each story involved another human life and their family and loved ones as well. I figured, if those strangers were able to do it, I could do it, too!

It's funny how when we face the unknown, we often stay

DOI: 10.1080/10570314.2014.927071

focused on ourselves. It's when we look outside of our own narratives and see so many others facing similar hardships that we realize we aren't alone in our journeys.

In a rush to get back to living my life, I (foolishly) ignored the concerns of my family and friends and flew down to Las Vegas to attend the annual Consumer Electronics Show. As I could almost have predicted, while there with my low resistance, even lower white blood cell count, and high exposure to rubbing elbows with thousands of people who had flown in from all over the world, I somehow picked up an unknown virus.

I'll spare you all the details of the crazy story, but essentially, I went to sleep after returning home *and didn't wake up.* I was found unconscious, my eyes rolled back, my body stiffened in complete rigor, and unable to breathe. Thinking my condition might be from an overdose, the medics who arrived at my house gave me a dose of NARCAN®, stuck me with a shot of epinephrine for good measure, and transported me to the hospital's ICU.

Multiple tests were performed by the medical staff, ultimately verifying that I had experienced a combination of septic shock, pneumonia, and respiratory failure. Any one of those three could have easily killed me, especially in my weakened condition from undergoing cancer treatment. None of them did.

I later learned that an old acquaintance of mine had died that very same week, from complications of the same strain of pneumonia that I had fought. *So,* I wanted to know, *why did I live? Why am I still here when I could have easily died?* My heart tells me there is a bigger purpose, something bigger than myself. The fact that I was found and saved at the last possible moment *and* able to recover from all three life-threatening conditions tells me that something amazing was set in motion. You can call it what you want, but I believe it was a miracle to have received help as I did. *It isn't about me,* but I do believe I have been allowed to endure so much so that I can draw upon these experiences to bless and encourage others.

CHAPTER FIVE
Clarifying Adversity

A friend once told me, "You should read what you write! If you want to write a book of fiction, read fiction. If you want to write about history, read books about history." That was when I began voraciously reading books about others who had faced adversity in different ways. Some authors wrote about how they fought cancer or lost a job, while others detailed the loss of a spouse or child due to an illness. Some even dealt with losing their marriage while trying to process the death of their child.

As I culled through the many books I had read, it occurred to me one day that I was only reading the stories of those who had had the courage, opportunity, and ability to write about their personal experiences. How many others would never have the opportunity to tell their stories?

The fact that you are reading this book likely means you (1) have faced significant adversity in the past, (2) are currently dealing with adversity, or (3) hope to gain insight so that you can support another person through an adverse time. The truth of it is, nearly every single person on this planet will face some kind of hardship or adversity during their lifetime, in a variety of ways, and in varying degrees of intensity and duration. Some may endure a horrific event that lasts only moments. Others may suffer from an adversity for decades—a chronic situation for which there is no end in sight.

Can one person's degree of distress be measured as more or less than another's? I don't believe so. What is intriguing to me is how we define the magnitude of impact from life's adversities. Our perspective of how bad something is will always be seen through the filter of comparison based on our previous experiences.

While all of us might experience some amount of adversity every day, the intensity and severity of our adversities are usually dissimilar. One person is simply irritated by the coffee stain on his slacks, while another is annoyed to the point of distraction and wraps his car around a tree. Each of us carries our own unique pain threshold and deals with it in our own unique way. Much of the time, we end up walking the journey alone, either because we are unable or unwilling to ask for the support we need, or because there is no one to ask.

How we interpret our adversity is similar to how we experience pain; again, our interpretations of feedback from pain receptors are relative—relative to other people's experiences with adversity, relative to our expectations of how life should be, and relative to our own previous pain. We subconsciously create a barometer, of sorts, and evaluate how challenging we perceive something to be by comparing it to our past experiences.

If you inadvertently step barefoot on a small Lego® building block, you might say it was an "8 out of 10" on a pain scale. However, when you go into labor to deliver your first baby, you would likely amend your previous assessment. I call that resetting your pain threshold. And so it is with personal adversity. With each experience, you reset and recalibrate your adversity threshold by interpreting how bad it was, based on a threshold that is continuously in flux.

When I started thinking about writing this book, I began sending occasional e-mails of encouragement to healthcare professionals who had been receiving my seminar updates. In my e-mails, I shared the potentially career-ending events I had gone through and how those experiences had eventually resulted in positive outcomes. A year later, I asked those same readers to complete an adversity survey to share their own experiences with adversity. A steady stream of e-mail replies began to pour in, filled with stories of heartache, perseverance, sorrow, joy, new-found strength, brokenness, wisdom, shifts in life-purpose, and clarity of direction.

Those stories provided invaluable insights which perhaps can only be fully appreciated by those who've endured such chaos in their lives. I realized that conducting interviews would allow me to dig even deeper and ask follow-up questions as well.

Over the next several months, I conducted dozens of interviews with brave individuals who hoped their experiences would inspire others facing similar circumstances. One person

I interviewed told me, "I just want what my family and I have endured to make a difference in someone else's life, for the wisdom we've gained from our experience to be a source of hope and healing for others who read your book."

So, what exactly is adversity? Merriam-Webster defines it as "a state or instance of serious or continued difficulty or misfortune[4]." The Cambridge Dictionary says it is "a difficult or unlucky situation or event[5]" while Dictionary.com describes it as "adverse or unfavorable fortune or fate; a condition marked by misfortune, calamity, or distress[6]."

As we know, an experience that would be considered an unfortunate incident in one person's life might be regarded as a calamity of unprecedented proportions in another's. No one can define what adversity is to you—*except you.*

I once was hiking a trail in Mt. Hood National Forest, when I came upon a ridge lined with young trees as well as the strewn remains of thousands of old-growth trees. I could tell the area had long been recovering from damaging hurricane-force winds from years earlier. Among the fallen and newer trees were many older trees that had survived the storm. One tree in particular—a Douglas Fir— reminded me of many of the people I encountered in my interviews. The tree had been violently forced over at a 45° angle causing some of its roots to be pulled

---

[4] Adversity. (n.d.). In Merriam-Webster. Retrieved December 13, 2019, from https://www.merriam-webster.com/dictionary/adversity
[5] Adversity. (n.d.). In Cambridge Dictionary. Retrieved December 13, 2019, https://dictionary.cambridge.org/dictionary/english/adversity
[6] Adversity. (n.d.). In Dictionary.com. Retrieved December 13, 2019, https://www.dictionary.com/browse/adversity

up and exposed to the elements. Rather than breaking, however, the tree was able to regain its foundation over time and change its direction, rising back toward the sky as it likely did before the storm. It was an odd sight, yet there was something profound in the shape of that rugged tree on that rocky path. The tree had been radically and irreversibly changed by the storm, but it had adapted itself to its new reality, continuing its quest for the sky above. It brings to mind Friedrich Nietzsche's famous words: "That which does not kill me, makes me stronger[7]." Adversity can push and push against us, sometimes leaving us bent like the tree with a new and different perspective.

The impact of adversity on an individual is increased exponentially when it hits a family unit. When tragedy strikes, the jumbled, preexisting complexities of a family's day-to-day connections and communication tend to be magnified by their mutual pain and loss. Each person in the family processes loss and emotion differently and the impact of their shared tragedy will be affected by the health of their relationship.

The most important thing to know is that regardless of its origins, we who face life-changing adversity all have the same set of options: We can give in to the adversity and give up, or we can continue forward albeit on an altered course, most likely finding out that we're better—smarter, stronger, more resilient—than we were before. We can lose everything, but no one can deny us our freedom to choose how we will react. Knowing the power that comes from that freedom is critical in our search

---

[7] Translated from German "Was mich nicht umbringt macht mich stärker." Nietzsche, Friedrich, Twilight of the Idols, or, How to Philosophize with a Hammer (German: Götzen-Dämmerung, oder, Wie man mit dem Hammer philosophiert) Published 1889.

for life's meaning.

Perhaps you have never been comfortable with change. For you, it's the consistency in your daily schedule that provides comfort, telling you from within, "Everything is okay. Nothing's changed." Over time, however, that consistency can also create such deep ruts in your path that adjusting to change becomes unusually difficult for you. Life is all about change. Sometimes it is self-directed. Other times, it's foisted upon us. How we perceive change and how we adapt to abrupt and unsettling departures from the lives we had envisioned will fundamentally impact our future realities.

My years of experience in the field of treating soft tissue injuries have given me a significant understanding of muscles and how they function. What I have witnessed firsthand is that a person's resilience in recovering from adversity is much the same as how a muscle responds to stress. Choosing to push through brings strength and flexibility, whereas lying down and giving up can lead to atrophy. Even people of advanced age can adapt and learn new ways of living and thinking because our brain tissues and thought processes are both malleable and fluid if we allow them to be.

Our readiness for change will always be predicated on our expectation of it. Expecting life to remain constant and unchanging, or assuming the context of our lives will adhere to our previously well-crafted plans, will result in broken dreams and unfulfilled expectations. Conversely, when we embrace the expectation for life to be a roller coaster of ups and downs and know that at some point adversity will find us, we automatically increase our resilience.

Picture an old car in the middle of a field which clearly

hasn't been moved in years. The rubber tires are sun-cracked and flat, the windows are covered with an opaque layer of green algae, and blackberry vines have wrapped themselves around the car as if making some kind of alien cocoon. The car couldn't go anywhere, even if its owner wanted it to. Now, picture an identical car speeding along a coastal highway, beautifully detailed and shiny. Those two cars are a great example of our preparedness for the inevitability of change in our lives—both the kind of change we have chosen and the change we couldn't have seen coming. If we keep our minds open and flexible in our expectations, we can take off in new directions when we want or need to. It's when we remain stagnant, unchanged for years, and fully entrenched in what has always remained the same, that we can't react and move in a new direction. Don't fear change. Prepare for it.

Self-Inflicted Adversity

I once knew a guy who was a chronic gambler. Over a period of twenty years or so, he lost his inheritance, his nest egg, and his earnings from making regular visits to various local casinos. His bills piled up because he couldn't pay them. He knew better. He was a smart fellow, a professional, yet he did this to himself. After losing everything that had been important to him, this man had to deal with many years of self-imposed adversity as a result of his own actions. He couldn't blame anyone or anything but himself—not his family, not God, not the 'unfairness' of life. He himself made the poor choices, and never considered the potential consequences of his actions.

Adversity can also be an internal war, where we are not at

peace with our own past choices and mistakes. Second-guessing ourselves or feeling guilty for the result of our poor decisions, we wallow in self-imposed torment because we cannot forgive ourselves. We're constantly wondering if life would be different had we made different choices.

If a woman loses her family because she had a romantic affair outside of her marriage, or if a man's house falls down because he didn't maintain it properly, they're both experiencing self-imposed adversity. Do we feel sympathy for them or do we adopt the standard *you-brought-this-on-yourself* attitude towards them? Probably the latter, and yet many of us could easily find ourselves in the same boat after making poor choices— even when we know it could end poorly.

Invisible Adversity

One of the magazines I read as a boy used to include a puzzle in the back in each issue. To solve the puzzle, you had to find what was different in the second picture compared to the first. By trying to solve those puzzles, I learned that even when we are purposely looking for something that might be missing or different, we don't always see it.

Not everyone's experiences with adversity are out in the open, or able to be identified by the casual onlooker. And when our adversity is unknown to others, we are deprived of the empathy and care from those who could otherwise be supportive.

When a police officer is killed in the line of duty, the brotherhood of police often band together to support the officer's family, ensure a hero's funeral, and bring attention to the loss. That is a rare exception to many people's experiences today, when—without external indicators to alert others— we're frequently left to face our adversity on our own.

Although we should treat everyone we encounter with the same respect, most of us might act with more grace if we knew while standing in line, for example, that the person who just cut in front of us had recently lost a child. Yet, in our culture today, we really don't have a universal way to make our grief known. Instead, we leave fragile, grieving parents to walk amongst us behind a cloak of invisibility, while we have little awareness of what they are enduring.

I know a young mom whose 16-year-old son, Carson, is autistic, intellectually impaired, non-verbal, and has an essential tremor. He also is handsome, which may sometimes be to his advantage but can also be a double-edged sword. Believing firmly that her child deserves and benefits from regular and frequent participation in the community, his mom takes him to restaurants, sporting events, theater, and church. People who don't know them have built-in expectations regarding the social skills of a tall, handsome teenager as opposed to those of a high-energy four-year-old.

But Carson's adversity is invisible—and his mother's is as well. People can't see the 'adversity' they are dealing with or even detect that an adversity exists at all, so they're blindsided. When Carson first sits down in a restaurant and begins making the unique sounds that enable him to communicate, people seated around them mistakenly assume he's being an obnoxious teenager, making unpleasant noises to be annoying. Then the food comes, and he eats it with his hands, which is the only way he can get his food into his mouth by himself. Horrified on-lookers become critical—of both the boy and his mom. Doesn't he know better? Can't she control her own child? Didn't any-one ever teach this kid any table manners?

Becoming familiar with Carson's story has opened my eyes to the possible stories hiding behind faces I interact with every day. The inconsiderate driver who cut me off in traffic, the di-sheveled loner at the bus stop staring intensely at the ground, or the woman sitting near me in a coffee shop, quietly crying into her handkerchief, all have narratives we invariably know nothing about.

Compound Adversity

As we know, adversity comes in all sizes, shapes, and colors. Something we must remind ourselves of is the possibility of compound adversity, which is simultaneous challenges occur-ring in someone's life. You have an automobile accident on the same day you're diagnosed with diabetes. Your neighbor's house burns down soon after he loses his mother. A friend's wife leaves him just when he loses his job. It can happen to an-yone.

How would you plan for a burial, look for a new place to live, replace your most basic necessities, comfort your children, and grieve the loss of your mate at the same time?

As I write this, I am days away from providing expert wit-ness testimony in an Arizona case in which a male massage therapist is being accused of sexual assault by one of his clients. I don't know the defendant personally, but I can tell you he is most certainly experiencing compound adversity. In addition to facing trial for a felony and potential incarceration, the state has suspended his license to work in his profession, and he has lost close to a year's income while his case slowly works its way through the legal process. He's dealing with the embarrassment of being publicly arrested and having his photo in the newspaper. His friends and family may even be wondering if the allegations about him could be true.

Finally, I can't write about compound adversity without remembering a former classmate. Teddy was the dreaded schoolyard bully from my elementary school days. Teddy loved to fight but never fought fair. He would hit you hard, knocking you off your feet. As you tried to get up and defend yourself, he would hit you again so you would lose your balance, fall down, and try to get up again. It is that decision—that will—to try to get back up on your feet that defeats the schoolyard bully I call compound adversity.

When Family is Your Adversity

Whether we like the idea or not, the experiences of our formative years will forever impact how we behave, make choices, and interpret our experiences in the years that follow. There is a Biblical verse that applies here: "Train up a child in the way he should go: and when he is old, he will not depart from it[8]." I believe that verse is interpreted in different ways for different people. Some readers may believe it refers to parents raising their children along a path of spiritual faith and observance.

---

[8] Prov 22:6 KJV

Another interpretation views the verse as a warning: Our children learn from what we say and by what we do.

Parents model behaviors to their children who are always observing and learning how to be in the world. Parents would be wise to consider that the next time they:

- Curse at the driver who just cut them off

- Consider bending the rules for their own gain

- Are about to lose their self-control in public

- Spend their weekly paycheck at the local pub or gambling casino

- Speak about others in a demeaning or critical way

- Abuse food, alcohol, medications, and other substances

- Begin to rationalize bad behavior—others' or their own

- Treat strangers in a rude or mean-spirited manner

Every moment we spend with our children is a lesson for them—a training in life. Some children will use their parents' questionable past choices as justification to perpetuate the behavior with their own behavior. Hearing about a felon's son being arrested for a crime would seem probable, right? The parent didn't teach his son to be a felon, but his son may have felt an implied permission to replicate his bad behaviors from just knowing that his own father had done it. Hopefully, most children today can recognize that behavior for what it is and do the opposite. Many do not.

I was born in 1962 and grew up in what my friends called a

Beaver Cleaver household. (You youngsters might need to Google that.) I had a father who worked forty hours a week, went to work at the same time each morning, and was home at the same time every evening for dinner. Dad was an active parent. He would do projects with me to teach me how things work. He taught me how to be a marksman and practice gun safety, taught me how to defend myself, and perhaps most importantly, he taught me how to be a loving and responsible parent.

My mother was a homemaker—she kept the house immaculate, always looked her best, and was a fantastic cook, having multiple-course meals prepared for each evening meal. Basically, Mom taught me how to keep up a house and take care of myself. I was mending lost buttons and ironing my own clothes while still in grade school. No one has ever had to take care of me since—as long as I'm healthy, that is.

Although I come from a loving and supportive home and haven't had the experiences others have had to suffer, I have observed brokenness in the homes of others due to a multitude of adverse family dynamics. Each story is different, and each situation needs a different response if the parties involved are ever to find healing and peace.

When parents act more like a school principal than they do a loving parent, the lack of communication, consideration, and effort to understand a child leads to distrust and despair on both sides. Both sides dig their heels in and refuse to "lose" the current argument—unwilling to back down from their belief that they are right and the other is wrong. Poor communication in families can often be attributed to selfishness and unmet expectations instead of a willingness to be vulnerable and honest with each other. This leads to broken-down relationships which can last for years or even a lifetime.

We've all seen some version of the following scenarios:

- A high school graduate with musical aspirations defies his father, who demands he enroll in law school. Following his own dreams of becoming a guitarist in a rock band goes against his father's wishes and will cost him the financial support he needs until he gets on his feet. Both are stubborn, and neither knows how to initiate a healthy dialogue about self-direction and fears.

- A woman is devastated when her parents pressure her to break off her relationship with a man whose social status isn't up to their standards. When they learn the couple has eloped, the parents cut off all communication, leaving her without the emotional support and family structure she had always leaned on.

- A child who has enjoyed unconditional love and support from her parents begins to question their devout religious beliefs. Rather than entering into healthy dialogue to address their child's changing convictions, the parents disown her, believing their actions are in the child's best interest.

- Both the children and the parents in a family turn to alcohol and drugs to numb themselves from the pain they are feeling after a major breakdown in communication. Rather than drawing closer as a family unit, they withdraw into separate worlds of escapism, which leads to even deeper, darker outcomes.

These and similar examples of family adversity can last for decades or be resolved quickly, depending on each side's maturity level and desire to keep the family intact.

Divorce also plays a central role in the kinds of challenging family dynamics that can often lead to adversity. From my own experience as well as from observing the relationships of others, I believe that divorce is frequently the result of miscommunication and/or unresolved anger—even if there is something more tangible that ultimately triggers the breakdown. When you realize how many parents fail to teach and model good communication skills, it is easy to understand the frequency with which this happens.

Also there is the belief that you deserve better than this. Americans, in general, believe we deserve to be happy. It's in our Constitution after all. Despite what may be a lifelong history of questionable behaviors and poor choices, we still believe we should have happiness. If you believe you deserve to be happy, you must acknowledge your responsibility, step up to the plate, and put in the work to make it happen. Otherwise, you will never possess the life skills necessary to grow a healthy relationship.

Jim's Story
I first met Jim Ladd when we were both in our early fifties. In addition to being the same age, if you were to look at the two of

us, side by side, you would see many other similarities: We have a similar build, the same hair color, the same sense of humor, and the same commitment to our families. However, our experiences growing up were distinctly different. While I was being raised in a wholesome household, Jim was not.

Over the years of our friendship, Jim has shared memories from his childhood and young adult years. His life story could fill a novel.

As a child of eleven, Jim's mother had been the victim of an attempted rape. She watched as both her parents tried to intervene but were shot, leaving her mother wounded and her father dead.

As a teenager, Jim's father had already impregnated the daughter of a wealthy Texan. The girl's angry father sent a hitman to threaten to kill the youngster who (wisely) never pursued the millionaire's daughter again. Eventually, he met Jim's mother, whom he married two weeks later. They were both 18.

Within three years, they had four children. Jim's dad had become a manufacturing plant manager, but when he learned that the firm's janitor earned more than he did, he quit his job and sold carpets for his brother-in-law's small flooring store, negotiating for increasing ownership of the business. He worked hard and grew the business to become one of the region's largest flooring operations, and he soon was a rich, young man. He was also an alcoholic and a habitual womanizer. Jim's life became an ongoing scenario of his parents yelling, screaming, throwing things at walls, and at each other.

"There was a lot of chaos in the family," Jim remembers.

When Jim's father was 36-years old, he was somehow wealthy enough to retire. He sold the company, but by then, the

IRS had caught on to his successful "side business" of selling carpet remnants for cash without reporting the sales. They assured him he would spend the rest of his life in prison. Then he found out he had cancer. He had surgery but the cancer grew back quickly. Knowing the IRS wouldn't give up, he opted to forego further surgery, and he died when Jim was just fourteen.

As we sat drinking coffee in Jim's office, I was trying to fathom what growing up in a family like that would feel like. I asked Jim how he thought it had affected him.

"I didn't know my family was unusual. You never really know when you're that young, but I later realized it after taking mental health classes in college. Then, as a married man, I also realized I had some distorted views on how life was supposed to go."

I interrupted Jim and asked how his mother had survived such a horrific trauma.

"I have a theory, based on this part of my story, that if a person doesn't go through an intentional and healthy recovery process and really deal with their experience, they get stuck somewhere. My mom, who's now 74-years old, is basically still eleven. She responds emotionally like an 11-year-old, she manipulates relationships like an 11-year-old, and she sees the world and makes decisions like an 11-year-old. I believe she doesn't know any better."

Jim smiled. "I definitely come from a bizarre family," he acknowledged. "I often feel like I'm the weirdo that came out of all that; but on the other hand, I've had some wonderful mentors. One of my dad's best friends came into my life immediately after Dad died. He saw to it that I had a strong paternal presence in my life. That changed everything." Jim paused to take a sip of coffee while I asked my next question.

"What have you learned from your experience which could be helpful for others?"

Without pause, Jim answered, "I absolutely believe that what happens to you is never as important as how you respond to what happens to you. I've learned over and over again to always hold the diamond up to a different light and find a different thing I haven't seen before. That's the gift my mentors gave to me. You are not what happened to you, you are not the failure of your past, you are not disabled or incapable, and God has not abandoned you. You just gotta' get up and keep going!"

He went on. "I always use the example of those old submarines that would launch a torpedo, and the torpedo would send out a radio signal to the target, and the signal would bounce back, and if the target had moved, the torpedo would change direction because it was responding to the feedback it was getting. That is what we do as human beings because God has wired us that way. But, if your antenna is broken, or if you're responding to the wrong target, you can get a million miles off course without even realizing it. You are instinctively responding to the feedback you are getting. Maturity is about understanding the feedback you are getting and interpreting it correctly."

I asked for Jim's observations of those who have demonstrated poor coping mechanisms.

"The indicator of poor choice is compulsion," he answered. "That's when someone says, 'I can't not do that.' Some compulsively drink, others compulsively do drugs, but we all have compulsions. And when I back up the lens on myself, I realize that is the issue. So, if all our behaviors are compulsive, they are symptomatic of something else. True freedom is when you can choose to act or not act ... speak or not speak ... eat or not eat. And if you don't have that freedom, you are bound. Once I got to that point back in my thirties when I realized I had stacks of compulsive behavior—like a junkie trading drugs all the time rather than being really free—it began turning on lights for me. I started to see how life works, to suddenly be able to navigate differently, to reject something even if I felt compelled to do it."

I asked Jim what advice he would offer to someone going through 'the impossible'—something they had never planned on.

"I don't think anybody should do life alone. Ever. You should never be without someone who's been further down the road than you who's helping you. My number one piece of advice is this: You've got to have somebody you can talk to who's already navigated what you're going through now.

"It's important to start asking lots of questions because the narrative you choose to embrace will determine your future. So, what story are you embracing? I retranslate the narrative of what I'm going through, then I interpret it correctly, and I start building the future that's in front of me. "

Today, Jim is the pastor of one of the largest churches in our region, although he doesn't have the persona most would expect from a man in his position. Despite his family history, Jim emerged into adulthood as a positive person who impacts and encourages people every week. He's got a big smile, a big heart, the ability to crack your spine with a hug, and is the most transparent and genuine church pastor I have ever met.

CHAPTER SIX
Adversity is Loss

When I began to interview people for this book, I expected to discover limitless categories into which every experience of adversity could be neatly identified, labeled, and organized. However, while sifting through my interview notes, I found one single common denominator connecting most of the stories: loss—loss of someone, loss of something, or loss of a vision.

My friend, Barry, for example, had become paralyzed in a high-speed motorcycle accident and had lost his ability to walk. Donovan's father developed Alzheimer's, losing his memories, his functioning skills, and his ability to find closure from the past. Very sadly, Don lost his wife and young daughter in a tragic fire.

While loss can take many forms—a job, a friendship, a home, a marriage, a physical ability, a loved one—some loss isn't as tangible, such as losing trust in someone or having your normal routine taken from you. When your day-to-day norm has been robbed from you, what you knew to be consistent is no longer. Life is now different, which can leave you with emotions ranging from unsettled to outright fright.

If you consider your own experiences with adversity, my hunch is that you will find loss in there somehow as well. With each story of adversity, dreams are dashed, plans are undone, and hopes are turned into hopelessness, at least for a time. Some people experience losses that are so significant the very direction of their lives is never the same. In those cases, a horrific event can often lead to a new and different future, which could never have been imagined beforehand.

Let's look at some different types of loss and how they can impact those who experience them.

Loss of a Job or Career

To some, getting fired or laid off from a job might be perceived as a blessing, a gift, or an opportunity. To others, the experience can be perceived as a staggering loss. We each have a choice as to how we interpret the experience. If you have ever had the experience of losing your job, how did you interpret what happened?

The loss of a job can be even more difficult for individuals who find their self-worth in what they do for a living. Their careers or job titles define their self-worth and confer their stature in society. For them, losing a job often feels as though they've lost their identity at the same time.

For most of us, the jarring impact of a job loss can be crippling, knocking us down, and leaving us with a diminished sense of hope. Then, trying to find a new job to rebuild one's self-respect can be a hollow and devastating experience. Sometimes, it isn't until we find the worth in ourselves that we might have the confidence to nail our next job interview and be a beacon of strength to our children, partners, and communities.

Loss of a Relationship

The end of any kind of relationship can be painful and emotionally challenging to process, regardless of how or why it happened. Adversity can come from the loss of a relationship, and, ironically, the loss of a relationship can be a direct side effect of adversity. And although the end of a friendship has happened to most of us in some way or another, unfortunately, the common experience doesn't diminish what can be a sad and painful void.

Over the decades, I too have lost relationships with both friends and family members. My childhood friend and playground buddy, Ben, was killed instantly when he dove off a dock and hit a submerged log. As a 9-year-old, this was a very difficult experience for me. I was too young to have to learn what that was like. My good friend was gone, and it would change me forever.

Years later, I befriended a fellow massage therapist named Jeff. We spent hours talking about fatherhood, work, and our personal lives. When Jeff became romantically involved with a woman whose proclivities were dark and in direct conflict with Jeff's values, our friendship began to suffer. He started to behave like an addict, unwilling to loosen his grip on a dangerous lifestyle. Over time, he drew increasingly embittered and self-conflicted, eventually pulling away from me, choosing his new lifestyle over our friendship. I soon found myself needing someone else to take Jeff's place as a friend.

Some relationships end when one person in the relationship has an experience the other is unable to share or empathize with. When my cancer "went rogue," I saw a noticeable shift in my friendships, which I could never have foreseen. One woman I was close friends with was hesitant to see me after my surgery and ultimately stopped all communication with me. Her sudden departure from my life was hurtful and left me feeling unappealing and rejected.

While the depth of connections we have with friends will ebb and flow over our lifetimes for different reasons, perhaps the most painful losses center around family relationships, such as:

- Death or disappearance of a parent or sibling
- Estrangement of a parent or sibling
- Renegade child who makes a new life in a different direction
- Family member who moves away
- Parent who has succumbed to the ravages of dementia or other cognitive disease

Loss of a Romantic Relationship

For most people, losing a romantic partner—particularly if they have been living together—can be especially devastating and life-changing. When that happens, it's easier to blame one's partner rather than blame oneself for the relationship ending.

Often, people are unable to see how their own behavior may have played a central role.

The romantic relationships in my life have been diverse, leaving me with a broad range of experiences. My shortest relationship was with Heather, a girl in my sixth grade English class. Our romance lasted from when I asked her to be my girlfriend at the end of second period until the start of our third period gym class. In a matter of moments, Heather had a change of heart. Our relationship had lasted twelve minutes.

As I moved forward into my adult years, the amount of time and emotion I was willing to invest in a relationship always seemed to have a direct correlation to the amount of emotional pain I had experienced in my previous breakup. The worse it had been, the more cautious and resistant I was in the following relationship.

Ultimately, each of us feels the loss of romantic relationships in our own way. Factors such as our age, previous relationship experiences, issues with intimacy, gender, and how we experience emotional connection, all can work to influence how we will respond to the end of a relationship. The specifics of why and how the relationship ended can affect our response as well.

It is usually helpful to take a pause after the loss of a relationship. Contemplating and acknowledging what it was you lost will go a long way in helping you understand your feelings. Despite the differences in how each of us experiences the pain of a relationship lost, the good news is that the tools we use to regain our emotional footing are more universal.

Relationships can bestow us with many benefits: safety, security, companionship, financial support, friendship, and someone with whom we can share the ups and downs of life. When we lose those benefits—as well as the relationship itself—the feelings of loss are intensified.

Relationships usually necessitate some degree of emotional connection. Our emotional intelligence will affect the balance in a relationship, as will the depth of the connection. The connection between two people can run along a diverse spectrum from healthy to dangerously unhealthy. Regardless of where the relationship lands along that spectrum, the connection is there.

The negativity we might feel around a past relationship will affect how we will remember it and even verbally describe it. As a cancer survivor, I find it helpful (if not a little weird) to compare a relationship with a malignant tumor. Stay with me here ... Some tumors have little to no connection to the surrounding tissue, while others are so deeply entrenched that removing them would require damaging surrounding tissue and removing whatever its "tentacles" had invaded.

When you lose someone you care about deeply, you seem to lose parts of yourself, yet the memories of your shared experiences remain. Each time you go back and revisit those memories, replaying them in your mind, allowing them to consume your thoughts, feels like pouring salt on your emotional wound. Those memories are like an old video cassette tape. We replay the video over and over without realizing we have the remote control in our hands, giving us the ability to press the pause button, or better yet, eject the tape.

Loss of a Marriage or Personal Partnership

Those who have experienced the breakup of a long-term, committed relationship often feel emotional devastation as multiple layers of complexity are added on to their experience. Promises are broken, trust is lost, dreams of the future are shattered—even spiritual beliefs can fracture. When a couple has children from their relationship, the damage can be even more profound.

The most difficult part of divorcing my children's mother has been the pain our decision ultimately inflicted on our three daughters. I'm sure that if you were to ask them, all three would tell you how they have been affected in the years since; but their stories are not mine to tell.

This book isn't about marriage, and I am certainly not an expert on the subject. What I do know is how the loss of our family unit impacted my former wife, our daughters, our families, our friends, and my business. It has now been sixteen years since the girls' mother and I divorced, and I now have a deeper understanding of what it means to be a good husband.

The most enlightening concept I have learned regarding marriage is that of a marriage of "commitment" as opposed to a marriage based on a "covenant." Whether we like it or not, our culture is one of quid pro quo agreements, and that includes many marriages. Basically, we give something in order to get something. And, when we give but don't get back what we expect, we feel our partner is in breach of our agreement. We compromise and sacrifice for our partners, and we expect to receive the same in return. We make our partners the priority and expect to become their priority as well. This describes a commitment-based marriage.

On the other hand, when you enter into a covenant-based marriage, you do so regardless of what you may or may not get back from your spouse. There are simply no conditions and no expectations. You are in it, no matter how fair or unfair it feels. Most parents feel this kind of unconditional love toward their children, irrespective of how the children behave or choose to live their lives.

Every relationship between two people is different. A relationship can be defined by a similar background, shared interests, day-to-day interactions, convenience, physical chemistry, or any combination of the above. These and other components of a relationship directly impact the level of satisfaction they individually feel and how much pain each would experience from a collapse of their commitment.

How committed you are in a relationship, combined with how committed you believe your partner is, will directly correlate to the level of loss you both would feel if the relationship were to end. If it is a relationship of convenience, the aftermath would likely be minimal, but if both partners are heavily invested, the emotional effects would be much greater.

One more point: A strong foundation is vital. Working in construction in the late eighties, I learned the importance of creating a strong foundation before proceeding to build something on top of it. Structures erected on top of poorly constructed foundations will eventually show signs of structural failure, which might even worsen over time. Building a strong foundation takes purposeful action and attention. Nothing is more important when building a new relationship.

Loss of Physicality

Losing something we have always taken for granted can be devastating, and that is especially true in regard to our physical abilities. Try getting through your day blindfolded, or with an arm tied behind your back, or without being able to walk. Those of us who get into accidents or require surgery and then must heal from them are certainly familiar with the inconvenience that loss of physical ability creates. It can even leave an amputee with psychological effects if they can't see beyond their perception of what the loss means to their way of life.

Losing half my tongue clearly affected my ability to speak as well as I did before—but I can still speak. I may have to work harder at it or warn someone they may need to listen harder, or even make specific accommodations to ensure that I'm being understood. Is it how I envisioned my life? Of course not. Is it fun? Certainly not. But does what I have to say still have the same value? By all means, it does. And does my attitude about it matter? Absolutely!

It is always impressive to see how adaptable, how confident, and how determined the human spirit can be in the face of physical loss.

After graduating from high school, my friend Barry went on a great adventure that took him thousands of miles throughout the western United States and Mexico. While riding his motorcycle in Oregon one day, he was getting impatient with the four slower cars who were ahead of him, and with no visible oncoming traffic, he decided to ignore the NO PASSING sign and pass all of them at once. As he blazed past them at more than 100 miles an hour, the driver in the front car made an abrupt left-hand turn and cut directly in front of him.

Barry's next memory was lying face down on an operating table as a team of spinal cord specialists was preparing to install hardware in his back to support his spine. Although he would never walk again, they needed to stabilize his spine so he would be able to sit upright.

A few weeks later, it was time for Barry to face the painful truth and make some choices as to how he was going to go forward with his life. He has always been a positive person. Now, his attitude was going to pay off and help him have a future.

"When I was going through this," he told me, "my positivity was infectious; it brought everybody up, especially me. There was no time for a pity-party. There was never a 'poor you.' Instead, it was all about getting me out of there! My positive support network, combined with my own positive attitude were what did it."

Barry continued sharing his recollections. "At one point, another patient who had been through something similar came to see me. He said something that really helped: 'You've got to set a major goal for yourself, and when you reach that goal, you'll know your motorcycle wreck is in your past. I decided I was going to go to Australia; that would be my goal."

After being in the hospital for a total of eight-and-a-half months, Barry used his newfound determination to fully embrace his physical rehabilitation work in order to get his strength back. He could see clearly there were many steps he needed to take, starting with dressing and transferring into his wheelchair by himself.

In the years since his accident, Barry has told his story to audiences throughout the United States in hopes of helping and inspiring others to face their own challenges. When asked what he learned from his experience, he thinks back to those days, years earlier.

"I was 22 when I crashed. I had already left home and traveled thousands of miles all over the west coast and Mexico, I was over six-feet tall, weighed over 200 pounds, and I did whatever I wanted to. I had been living on my own, and I didn't really need anybody else.

"And then, I found myself in this situation where I couldn't do anything by myself, and I had to always rely on someone else. It was even harder because I wanted to prove to myself that I could do it. One of my biggest challenges after coming to terms with my new physical reality was asking for help.

"I was afraid that asking for help meant I was weak, but then I realized that that thinking was absolutely wrong. That is one of the biggest reasons I've been successful. Asking for help has opened up the world for me, helping me take on challenges without as much fear.

"Another interesting advantage I had was knowing I had done this to myself. I had no one else to blame, so no anger to carry around with me. I simply had to take responsibility for what had happened and forgive myself. But even if somebody else had been at fault, I would have forgiven them. It's like how when Nelson Mandela was leaving prison, he stopped, turned around, and forgave his captors. Unforgiveness isn't worth holding onto. It's not positive.

"Yes, there are complications that come with being a wheelchair user. But everyone has complications in life. Everyone has their wheelchair! Mine is just more obvious, more visible. If you don't let things stop you, they won't, I bungee jump in my wheelchair, and I water ski, snow ski, and skydive. I've learned to fly airplanes, been a competitive wheelchair racer, got married, had children, and I drive a hotrod. I do the things I want to do. When someone says, 'You can't do that!' I say, 'Why not?'"

Almost three years after becoming paralyzed in a motorcycle crash, Barry finally made it to Australia and New Zealand with the help of a good friend.

Loss of a Child

Before interviewing anyone, I already knew that the loss of a child was about as difficult as it could get, that no other adversity could come close to that kind of trauma.

Finally, my interviews began. Over a period of several weeks, I talked with dozens of parents who had each experienced the tragic loss of a child, or in a few cases, children. While the loss was common among the parents, how it happened was not. The causes of death ranged from diseases and suicide to accidents and gun violence. Each story of anguish, loss, enduring pain, and often guilt was as unique as it was heart-wrenching to hear.

As I interviewed each of the parents, my heart ached as I listened to each story, and after the last interview, I was emotionally spent. Even years after their child's passing, I could still see the excruciating to paralyzing pain that those parents continued to carry.

During one interview, a young father told me about an exchange he had had with a woman in his support group. When he learned she had lost her entire family twenty-five years earlier, he pleaded with her, "Please! Tell me this gets easier!"

"No," she answered, "it never gets easier, but you get stronger."

One thing the fifteen parents had in common was how they viewed their loss and their healing process afterward. Each in their own way told me that while the wound from losing a child eventually healed, the scar forever remains on a parent's heart, and their loss changes them forever.

Another response I saw among several of the parents I met was the desire to find some meaning in their child's death and to use it as an inspiration to reach out and benefit others who were hurting.

When I was in high school, my friend Lori Baker and her grandmother were killed in a Christmas Eve house fire. Now, reflecting back on the experience while I was interviewing him, Lori's father told me, "Lori's mom and I were resolved that something good would come from it. We found ourselves encouraging others who were mourning a loss. We opened our home one evening a week to inspire and encourage other kids who had been impacted by knowing Lori." The Baker family's life had changed, and they were determined that they would turn their adversity around so it would be a blessing to others.

Another set of parents had lost their seven-year-old son to a rare form of cancer. They were determined to take their agonizing adversity and turn it into a positive. As they faced the first anniversary of his death, they started an annual bike ride and fundraiser in their son's name. It's been more than twenty years, and they've raised close to a half-million dollars to benefit pediatric cancer research.

Here are some other stories...

Mike's Daughter, Selena

Mike lost his oldest daughter, Selena, in an automobile collision when she was twenty years old and a junior at Washington State University studying architecture. She was a passenger in a van with other students when the driver didn't see the black ice on the road, and their van went careening across the median into oncoming traffic. All the passengers survived except Selena, who died on impact.

Within a few months of Selena's passing, Mike's wife, Tanya, heard about The Compassionate Friends (TCF), a support group for parents who've lost a child lead by fellow bereaved parents who had been specially trained to facilitate meetings.

Tanya said, "I'm going," Mike recalled, "and you're taking me."

Mike doubted whether a support group would help him. As he explained to Tanya, "Men and women are wired differently and we process things in a different way. At one moment, you might need a hug and someone to sit beside you on the sofa, while I need to keep busy, go out and fix the car, or mow the lawn. I'm not sure about going."

But Tanya persisted. "For the first several meetings, it was hard for me," Mike said, "but I went because Tanya wanted to. She got a lot out of it. Ironically, after a couple of years, when she was ready to stop going, I was finding it helpful and wanted to continue."

Mike elaborated, "There was this wonderful woman who ran the meetings who had lost two daughters. Whenever we arrived, she always greeted us with a big smile. She would sit down with us, wanting to listen, wanting to help, and I came away with hope. I was always surprised at meetings to hear people laughing who seemed to be okay. I didn't know how it was possible, but with everyone's support, I eventually started to think I might get through it, too."

After a few years, Mike became the co-leader of his group. He has since worked with hundreds of parents, family members, and loved ones left behind following the loss of a child. The experience has given him valuable insights through his observations and personal connections.

"For most people, the death of a child can do one of two things," Mike told me. "It can harden you, and you withdraw and become bitter and often remain that way. But people who come to a support group, read books on bereavement and get involved in their church or community activities often end up better people. They become more sensitive to others and what's important in life.

"There is no formula. I can't promise someone that in six months they'll be at a certain point. We are all different. For months there is no joy. Things that used to bring you joy don't anymore. You're exhausted. You find it difficult to concentrate. You're numb. In the second year, people begin to understand what they're dealing with, that their child isn't coming back. That second year can be even worse for some people because the numbness has worn off. Recovery is a wavy line which goes up and down but generally trends upward. It's a rollercoaster.

Mike said, "If there is ever a time in your life that you would benefit from counseling, it is after losing a child. Seek out qualified, professional grief counselors, specifically ones who have lost a child themselves. You need someone you can call at two or three in the morning when you can't sleep.

"Bereaved parents need to adjust their expectations of themselves and avoid saying, 'I should be able to play golf with my friends. I should pay more attention to my spouse or my kids.' This is a time in your life when the shoulds don't apply.

"Many parents go through a period of blaming themselves for their child's death. 'I should have been there. I could have prevented this. I should have known. I should have called him. I should have found a different doctor,' and so on. Parents mistakenly think they should have had 'godlike' qualities, but they don't. We can't put that kind of blame on ourselves.

"Finally, I had always assumed that the stress and strain of a child's death would be the end of most marriages, but my assumption was wrong. When couples actively work to strengthen and fortify a marriage before adversity's impact, it helps you survive when something goes wrong. I believe if there are serious problems in the relationship, losing a child can easily be the tipping point. It's like a vase that looks fine, but if there is a crack you can't see, and somehow it gets jarred, it shatters. For most marriages which are healthy and strong, although it's not easy, the two partners can help each other, and they can come out stronger."

Allen's Daughter, Tammy

Twenty-five years ago, Allen's 30-year-old daughter, Tammy, died of a drug overdose. Like Mike, Allen is a group leader for a chapter of The Compassionate Friends. He's an electrical engineer in a successful business he started in his garage fifty years ago. Over the years, Allen has gained considerable wisdom and insights into the experience of losing a child. He enjoys his work and enjoys his life, and he still misses his daughter.

He shared with me that Tammy died while he was away on a business trip.

"If only I had not been away," he lamented. "Would she have called me before doing that to herself? Who knows, but I was away and shouldn't have been. My guilt was enormous. I know there is no rational answer for feeling guilty, but what if I could have done something to prevent it?"

"Virtually everyone feels guilt," he says. "I carried that burden for ten years. We beat ourselves up. The reality is, none of us purposely intended to hurt our children. We loved our children, and we meant well for them, but eventually, we must accept the reality that life is not perfect, we are not perfect, and accidents happen."

Allen and I talked about his observations of others who have worked through their own grief process.

"At the time of a loss, we go through a stage of incredible trauma," he told me. "It's like having an arm cut off. It doesn't hit you at first. Only after the pain and trauma begin to subside, which takes a period of time, do the reality and the longer-term grief come to the forefront."

One of the women in Allen's support group tried—unsuccessfully—to end her life several years ago, but eventually, she made her way back to living a productive life. Allen shared, "She went from the trauma and most intense pain, to completely losing the will to live, to reconnecting back to her life and to the future.

The same can happen to the vast majority of us over time, but that time must be measured in terms of years—not weeks or months—to be realistic. A bereavement counselor who works with Allen says her rule of thumb is about five years, but everyone is different.

"People must also understand it's a gradual transition; you don't wake up one morning a changed person. It happens so slowly you don't always realize it. What's most important to hold on to is that the depth of your grief is a measure of your love for the child you lost."

I asked Allen his advice on processing grief in a healthy way, and he offered, "The techniques vary from person to person. But one thing we all need is to have something in our lives that has a purpose, both in the short and the longer term, something for us to focus on.

"We never quit wanting our children back," he said, "and we never stop having triggers which can result in pain at any point in time. We learn to balance what we have lost with loving what we still have.

"And then one day, something will feel good when you don't expect it. It could be a hug or seeing new growth in the garden, or the beauty of a sunset. You start to realize that you feel something other than pain for the first time in years."

Austin's Son, Liam

Austin and his siblings were raised by a sadistic, abusive father. As soon as he was of age, Austin left home, enlisted in the Air Force, and got stationed on the opposite side of the country to put as much distance between his father and himself as possible.

Not having had a normal childhood took its toll. It wasn't long before Austin was court-martialed for possession of illicit drugs and sent to jail. When he received a Bad Conduct Discharge from the Air Force, his wife, Ava, divorced him and left him with their two-year-old son, Liam.

Years passed as Austin did his best to raise his son, but he had never learned how to be a parent. As Liam grew older, he hung around with a tough crowd who were a poor influence on him. He was in and out of trouble regularly and served endless time in several prisons.

One morning on his way to work, Liam was pulled over for having fake tabs on his car. When the patrolman ran a background check and realized there was a warrant out for Liam's arrest, Liam became agitated. He shot the officer with a 25-caliber handgun and the officer returned fire, killing him on the spot, there on the freeway off-ramp.

Later, when the patrolman was describing to Austin what had happened, the news felt like a kick in the chest.

"I walked around in a daze," he remembers. "All I knew was that my son was dead. Then I got into a bad place. I drank more. I smoked more dope. I started doing meth. People who cared about me would ask what they could do, but I didn't even know what I needed. I had no support of any kind; I had nothing. Eventually, I lost my job and then my house to foreclosure. To numb myself, I stayed high for a week at a time, and then I'd sleep for a couple of days and start again. I didn't care about anything. When I started contemplating suicide, I went to an in-patient mental health facility where I did get some help.

"I took a few side jobs and started having a more normal life. But I was so full of regret, consumed with what I could have done or should have done. What if I had been there more? Taken more interest in his life, or set a better example? I had hit rock bottom. I needed something. So I turned to God.

"I had the same questions for God that any parent would have. Why Liam? Why did it have to be him? I was choked with guilt. I was such a terrible father, and he didn't have a chance.

"There was a church up the street where they were very accepting, and I started to attend regularly. I would sit there during the service each Sunday and just cry. I had a lot of sorrow, a lot of pain and misery, and I couldn't forgive myself for what had happened. I felt I had brought this all on myself and deserved to be punished.

"The church started offering a twelve-step support group called Celebrate Recovery. The guys in the first meeting were all opening up about their personal stories, so I decided to share, too. Then it just all poured out, but they didn't condemn me. They accepted me.

"I also joined a grief group at the church and started meeting other people who had lost children. Everybody had a different story, and we all were processing our grief differently.

"All these years later and I'm now clean and sober, and a single father again, raising my daughter, Tara, on my own. You know, with Liam, I messed up as a father, but with Tara, I've done it right. I've bought a house, met a nice woman in church, and remarried. Everything I had lost, I believe God restored."

Austin had lost everything but had regained all that and more. While his losses were restored, Austin said, "They can never be replaced. The loss of one child can never be made up with a new child. That emotional limb will forever be severed. However, a new limb can bring new purpose and more fullness to a life which before had merely consisted of chaos and pain."

As my conversation with Austin drew to a close, I asked if

he would be willing to share some wisdom he might have gained through his experiences. What would he want other parents to know?

"Don't miss an opportunity to tell your kids you love them," he said. "Don't miss the opportunity to go to their events and be there for them, because they need and deserve that. And you need and deserve that. I missed those opportunities with Liam, but I learned from it, and I won't miss them this time around."

CHAPTER SEVEN
Interpreting Obstacles

It is strange how easily we tend to focus on the things we don't have rather than on what we do have. When something is denied or taken from us, or when we don't get what we expected to achieve or receive, we too often interpret it as a negative, or worse, a personal failure. We may become angry, complain, blame somebody, or obsess about how much better our lives would be had we not suffered this loss.

There is another way of looking at that loss, however, whereby we consider it as perhaps a *positive* opportunity. Without exploring that perspective, I believe we're missing out on an entire set of options and possibilities in our lives. If we are able to see it as *dodging a bullet*, we can perhaps see the freedom it affords us rather than the limitations that missed "opportunity" may have brought with it.

Our negative interpretations of life's events are often due to our limited, myopic perspective. We are unable to step far enough back to see that something good might actually be the result of our situation. I vividly remember losing my beautiful home after my business failed. Next was the repossession of my BMW. I can still feel the queasiness I experienced as my right hand politely shook the repo man's hand while my left hand gave him my car keys. Looking back at that moment still brings a smile to my face because of the freedom that I was gaining in place of what I was surrendering—although I didn't know it yet.

The truth is, these losses left me in better shape financially than I had been previously. Thanks to the *Great Recession*, both my home and my car had gone way down in value and were now worth only half of what I still owed on them. From the experience, I learned that I didn't need to be angry. I was experiencing "loss" yet simultaneously finding freedom. These seemingly "catastrophic" events had loosened the shackles on my financial future. Perspective was everything.

Remember the story of how we got the lease in the hospital for my massage school? How I came to start a vocational school at all was the direct result of a *significant* obstacle.

The year before we finalized the lease for our initial massage school location, I had heard that I could use the multi-purpose room in Capital Medical Center's "Physician Pond" for free because I was a medical office tenant. Free rent! I sat down with the landlord to schedule my classes, deciding which were the specific evenings I would need the room.

"Great!" he said when I was done. "Just one last detail: The woman who teaches yoga here will need to agree to change her time slot in order to accommodate your schedule. You will need to give her a call to work it all out."

The next day I called the yoga instructor to ask if she would be open to moving her night so I could start my school. I explained how amazing the school was going to be and how it was a dream I had had for the past decade. Yet, no matter how I explained it, she could not see my vision or grasp the incredible significance of the situation. If she could only see how important this school was to the community ... to the profession ... *to me!*

"No" was the only answer she would give me. Just "No."

I was devastated, and now my school would not have access to this "perfect" classroom. Sure, it was tiny, but it was free! It did not matter to me that the space offered us no storage options for our school supplies and equipment, that the classroom layout wasn't optimal, or that we would not be able to display anything on the walls. It was my plan, and now it was being derailed by a yoga teacher!

I licked my wounds and simmered in frustration for several days until I noticed an availability sign for a brand new, local commercial property. It was right across the street in a medical park and ready to be built-out by a contractor precisely as we would need it. Even better, it had storage space, it could accommodate more students, and we could even display our learning materials on all the walls!

Thinking about it, I realized this property was truly perfect for what we needed. The added space would provide many opportunities to make our school the best it could be—an exceptional school—from which we would graduate exceptional, well-rounded, skilled students. My frustrating, insurmountable hurdle from a week earlier had actually turned out to be a blessing to my business. It was *because* of that obstacle that I ended up with more students, more staff, and a better location for our school!

There are times in everybody's lives when it feels like we are under attack from forces beyond our control, pummeling us relentlessly, chipping away at us mentally and physically, even undermining our dreams. In hindsight, we're often able to see how those difficulties led to an outcome we never expected, resulting in wisdom and understanding to bless and encourage others.

Perspective can help us realize that ultimately, what we thought was an obstacle may not have been an obstacle at all, but a way to take us on a better path to our ultimate destination. Let's say you need to drive from Point A to Point B, but there's a huge mountain blocking your way. What do you do? You drive around it. Yes, you have to drive nearly four times the distance, but the scenery is beautiful, the roads are safer, and you do finally get to where you need to be.

Now, think of this possibility: Along your drive, you spontaneously make a stop at a small convenience store, where you end up buying a book, which gives you a new concept to think about, which ultimately puts your entire future on a brand new path.

Instead of interpreting the mountain as an obstacle that holds you back and keeps you from your dreams, it could, in truth, be divine intervention, gently guiding you in a radically different direction you couldn't have previously imagined.

Perspective is a choice, directly related to the concepts of optimism and pessimism. As it has been said before in numerous ways, pessimism is seeing the difficulty in opportunity, while optimism is seeing the opportunity in difficulty.

As I was researching for this book, I came across a remarkable woman named Wyanne Thompson, who had survived the same type of cancer I had, with the same idiopathic cause. Wyanne's cancer was more invasive, however, requiring a more radical surgery. Not long after I had to have half of my tongue removed, Wyanne lost her *entire* tongue. While I was complaining I had lost most of my ability to taste, Wyanne will never eat again. To this day, she is unable to swallow and gets all of her nutrition through the same type of abdominal PEG tube I had briefly had. I also had complained about losing some lymph nodes in my neck, but Wyanne lost over three times as many along with muscle tissue, leaving her with a visible deformity in her neck.

Perspective is everything, and Wyanne inspires me. Every morning she starts her day in prayer, giving thanks for the privilege of another day on this earth. She gives thanks for everything she is blessed with, keeping what she *has* at the forefront of her thoughts rather than dwelling on what she no longer has. Today Wyanne lives a vibrant life as an artist[9], author, and instructor, traveling the world and living her dreams.

As most of us have learned, unique or uncommon hardships can easily garner the attention and sympathy of others, while more common types of adversity are easier to dismiss. Yet

---

[9] See Wyanne Thompson's art on her website: https://www.wyanne.com

whatever the hardship is, regardless of its intensity for the person enduring it, it is new and overwhelming, often leading them to a place of feeling isolated and alone.

Over the years I have worked with thousands of clients enduring their own personal struggles and have watched as they navigated their recoveries from injuries and other traumas. I have seen over and over again how the way someone interprets their experience directly affects or even creates their new reality.

Let me give you an example. Two different women have been robbed by the same thief on the same night, in the same neighborhood, in the same manner. Both victims have lost their valuable jewelry, TVs, and sound systems. Yet despite all the similarities, their healing from the unsettling experience will be determined by how each woman processes and interprets the event. A year later, one of the women might still be a nervous, broken shell of her former self, while the other is stronger, empowered, and even helping others who have gone through similar trauma.

Why is one person stronger and empowered while the other is emotionally broken, unable to move on? Is the difference based on one's genetic makeup? Their religious views? Perhaps how they were raised or taught by example? I believe it is something else altogether.

While we don't always have the ability to change the paths our lives take or our individual circumstances, we always have a choice regarding how we react to a situation. The fact is, *we do have a choice*, and, it's a skill that can be taught, practiced, and learned so we can emerge stronger and more positive.

Perspectives and Perceptions

If I hold my hand up to my face and cover my eyes, my hand blocks my view of nearly everything around me. If I hold my hand at arm's length, however, it only blocks a tiny percentage of what is around me.

The more we concentrate and focus on a form of adversity that is present in our lives, the more it prevents us from seeing the incredible blessings that we have.

Our perspective is also directly related to our *vantage point* when we consider our experiences. A great analogy is the seat you have at a football game. While the referees have the advantage because they can consult play-by-play recordings taken by multiple video cameras strategically placed around the field, most of the fans only see the game from their singular perspective from the stands.

How we interpret our past, how we interpret our partner's words during a conversation, or how we decipher the events we are experiencing in the present moment ... all of our perceptions of life's events are shaped and impacted by our perspective. As long as our emotional wounds have yet to heal, they can smudge our "camera's lens," leading us to perceive events through that filter of the past and alter what we believe to be true. We can choose how we interpret events and make the decision to step back and view them in a new way, without the filters we have collected from our past emotional wounds and negative experiences.

Cognitive Reframing

Events which take place in our lives aren't necessarily defined as good or bad, nor do they come with any inherent message or meaning. They just happen. Drawing on our past experiences, we will assign them meaning based on how we interpret them. If a farmer's cornfield is destroyed by fire, the farmer can view the event as a negative one, thinking he just lost his field of corn, or a positive one, realizing his cornfield soil has now been enriched for the following season!

One of the most powerful tools we can use when recovering from adversity involves the process of *cognitive reframing*. Essentially, cognitive reframing takes place when our mindset changes how we view an event, regardless of whether the change is a positive or a negative one. Mental health professionals who practice Cognitive Behavioral Therapy use the technique of *cognitive reframing* to help their patients look back and revisit specific experiences and learn to see them from a more positive and healthy perspective, thereby redefining the meaning, value, and impact of the experience.

Not everyone who is sad can simply decide to be happy. That said, wanting to change is a *cognitive* decision. Essential to Cognitive Behavioral Therapy is the understanding that our thoughts direct our emotions, and our emotions direct our behaviors. We can't typically control every event that happens in our lives, but we can definitely control our reaction to it.

We already know that we view our life experiences through individual filters based on our past experiences. Then, we evaluate the event as either a positive or a negative one, and we can do that either consciously or subconsciously. If our filters lead us toward negative thoughts, and if those thoughts become negative emotions, the result can be acting out with negative, unhealthy behaviors. Alternatively, someone who wants to view every event in his life as a positive might delude himself and remain too long in an unrealistic and overly optimistic scenario. He dismisses others' concerns and tries to justify his willingness to see his situation the way he does.

Those unrealistic perceptions are the result of an altered view of reality, known as *cognitive distortion.* These skewed ways of seeing things can include seeing the world as either black or white, jumping to conclusions, overgeneralizing, discounting what is actually positive, blaming others, and worrying about things that would never likely happen.

If a woman is unable to reframe her thoughts on her own, she can seek out the help of a qualified Cognitive Behavioral Therapist. The therapist will guide her through a positive reframing process known as *cognitive restructuring.*

Therapists utilizing cognitive restructuring usually follow a multi-step approach, which varies from therapist to therapist. The steps often include:

- Having their client begin with some form of calming, mental relaxation such as intentional breathing or meditation

- Identifying the situation and determining what specifically triggers their response

- Assessing their mood and trying to describe it

- Determining their automatic reactions to the mood experienced

- Writing down the evidence that both supports and contradicts their thoughts

- Reviewing the supporting and contradicting evidence and comparing the two for a balanced view of the situation

- Considering alternate thoughts to adopt when thinking about the event

- Monitoring their mood by writing down how they feel

EMDR

When a relatively new therapeutic technique consistently shows effective results 90 percent of the time, yet the professionals aren't quite sure why, it's worth exploring.

EMDR, or Eye Movement Desensitization and Reprocessing, is just such a technique, and it is being used by mental health professionals nationwide, with an effectiveness that is both significant and consistent. This is especially true when it is used for treating people with adverse Post Traumatic Stress Disorder (PTSD) and other emotional traumas.

Essentially, EMDR is a method used by therapists to help clients determine which stressful memories they may need or want to address, and then work on eliminating or changing their perception of those memories. The therapist asks the client to think about a particular memory and the negative ways the memory makes them feel about themselves. At the same time, the client is receiving *physical stimulation, which is continually alternating from one side to the other side, back and forth.* The stimuli could be the therapist's finger moving back and forth, or a mechanical light moving from side to side, or even the therapist tapping the client's two sides alternately, perhaps on the hands or knees. The therapist will repeat the routine several times, each time having the client consider a different aspect of the trauma while also being distracted by the stimuli.

The reason mental health practitioners believe this seemingly simple technique works is because when people focus on a specific aspect of their trauma while they also are distracted with the alternating stimuli, the neurons reconfigure themselves and the buried traumatic memory gets unstuck, reprocessed, and then moved over to where it belongs in the prefrontal cortex[10]. The entire process leaves the brain desensitized to the trauma and allows the client to recall the trauma without the intense response it would previously conjure.

While some think EMDR is nonsense, numerous studies[11] on the use of EMDR on those experiencing PTSD show remarkable outcomes ranging from 70-100%, and the U.S. Department of Veteran Affairs concurs. On their website, they state, "EMDR has the strongest recommendation for being an effective treatment in most clinical practice guidelines for the treatment of PTSD[12]."

---

[10] Luber, M., Fernandez, I., Zabukovec, J., Hase, M., Cole, J. W., Faretta, E., Farrell, D., Reid, K. O., Luca, Bertino, G. N., Manuela, Carletto, S., Kavakçı, Ö., Cattaneo, M. C., Chiorino, V., Roveraro, S., Salerno, R., Chiorino, V. & Salerno, R. (2018). Forematter. Neurobiological Foundations of EMDR Therapy. In M. Luber (Ed.), Eye Movement Desensitization and Reprocessing (EMDR) Therapy Scripted Protocols and Summary Sheets, (pp. xxiii-xxvii) Springer Publishing Co.
[11] Shapiro F. (2014). The role of eye movement desensitization and reprocessing (EMDR) therapy in medicine: addressing the psychological and physical symptoms stemming from adverse life experiences. The Permanente journal, 18(1), 71–77. https://doi.org/10.7812/TPP/13-098
[12] U.S. Department of Veteran Affairs. (2020). Eye Movement Desensitization and Reprocessing (EMDR) for PTSD. Retrieved April 30, 2020 from https://www.ptsd.va.gov/professional/treat/txessentials/emdr_pro.asp

I could probably fill the rest of this book by listing numerous other behavioral modalities used to cope with adversity. I'll simply say that having an open mind to explore those techniques is the first and most crucial step toward true healing.

CHAPTER EIGHT
The Power of Thought on the Body

If you ever have the opportunity to assist in an autopsy, be prepared for your innocence to be lost. Exploring the insides of a human body will forever change the way you think about your own body and how it works.

First of all, it brings you face-to-face with your own mortality. You realize how fragile and vulnerable our systems are and how many things can go wrong and change our lives forever. What is most unforgettable is understanding the role of the brain. Not only does your brain keep everything working, but it also carries around your consciousness. And while your physical body isn't necessarily who you are, you wouldn't have many friends without one.

I vividly remember standing in the county coroner's autopsy lab, holding in my hands the brain of someone who had died just the night before. It gave me a sense of wonder I have not experienced before or since. From a physiological perspective, the brain is a gray, spongy, wet ball of tissue that sort of resembles miniature human intestines, neatly folded into someone's skull. From a functional perspective, the brain is stupefying. It's like a supercomputer which is on the job every second we are alive, working to keep the body functioning behind the scenes without our even realizing it.

Think about the brain as you would an incredibly complex vehicle, and you are simply the passenger. Once you set a destination for yourself, you barely have to think about all the things your brain is going to have your body do in order to get you to where you want to go. In fact, it's going to quietly handle all the details while you sit back and enjoy the sights!

Each day of your life, your brain is multi-tasking on an astronomical scale. It is ensuring that your heart beats at the precise rate necessary to provide sufficient oxygen-rich blood to your muscles and other organs. It's monitoring and controlling your vascular pressure by engaging and releasing the tiny musculature in your arteries. It's operating the intricate actions in your eyes while also taking in new visual data—and interpreting it—so you can drive a car, play tennis, do your work, or detect a subtle nuance of expression on somebody's face. It's keeping you breathing whether you're awake or asleep. If all that weren't enough, your brain is, at any given moment, making hundreds of micro-adjustments on your behalf while you are busy doing something else.

At one time in your life, you've probably read this thought-provoking quote on someone's office wall: "Whether you believe you can do a thing or not, you are right[13]." The event described here proves it.

Before May 6, 1954, no human had ever been able to run a mile in less than four minutes. Four minutes was the unwavering, unbeatable record. It seemed that regardless of an athlete's age, training techniques, current weather conditions, or any other variable, it couldn't be done. Until it was! On a cold and wet afternoon at Oxford University, a 25-year-old medical student ran a mile in 3:59[14], which was six-tenths of a second under the four-minute time. What wasn't supposed to be possible suddenly was, and it opened the floodgates for others to duplicate the feat. In fact, it took only forty-six days for another runner to do it in 3:57.9. In the years since well over a thousand runners have surpassed that number, and today's record stands at 3:43[15].

The moral of the story? If we think something is possible and we set a goal to achieve it, our mental constraints are released, and we then *believe* we can reach our goal. Will positive thoughts make an amputee's limb grow back? Not likely. How we think affects us, but it won't make us live forever or be able to leap over tall buildings.

Our body responds to what we choose to believe is true. Our beliefs affect our actions as well as our physiology, even down to the cellular level. When I was in college, a friend trained me in Tae Kwon Do. Phil was a black belt himself, and

[13] Similar variations of this quote have been attributed to numerous authors. https://quoteinvestigator.com/2015/02/03/you-can
[14] https://www.guinnessworldrecords.com/records/hall-of-fame/first-sub-four-minute-mile
[15] https://www.guinnessworldrecords.com/world-records/fastest-run-one-mile-(male)

when he said he was going to put his hand through a wooden board, he did.

"You can do this," he assured me. "You throw one punch, aimed six inches *behind* your target, and that one will be enough." Phil was so confident that I could do it that he made me confident as well. He had made me *believe* I could do it. And I did it.

Most of us have heard or read about people with multiple personalities—a rare condition that is more common among women—which health professionals refer to as dissociative identity disorder. I have read about how common it is among people with this disorder to have different personalities with varying physiological features. Some personalities within the same individual have different reactions to medications, for example, while one's brain wave activity differs dramatically from her alternate personality. Some switch out their prescription glasses when different personalities emerge. (Optometrists have even confirmed changes in visual acuity from one personality to another.) What especially amazes me is the *non-diabetic* person whose alternate personality *is diabetic.* That tells me their body chemistry actually changes because that personality *believed* she has diabetes.

Our beliefs create a physiological response in our body under directives from our brain. It's what is known as the *body-mind connection.* Hypnotists have been able to place a finger on the forearm of a person who is in a deep state of hypnotic suggestion and tell them their arm had just been burned with a hot iron[16]. Within moments, a red welt can appear due to an

---

[16] Grosso, Michael. (2007). Irreducible Mind: Toward A Psychology for the 21st Century. Lanham, MD: Rowman & Littlefield Publishers

immediate histamine reaction. The person believes the burn is real, and their body responds appropriately.

Countless studies have shown that chronic stress and anxiety can suppress our immune systems, making us susceptible to illness, encouraging the progression of infectious diseases, impairing our body's response to vaccines, and lengthening the time it takes a wound to heal. Research in the field of psychoneuroimmunology[17] confirms that positive thoughts, emotions, expectations, and attitudes can have a powerful impact on our health and actually enhance our immune system[18]. Relaxation techniques, stress-reducing activities, and therapeutic intervention have been clinically proven to boost our natural killer cells, shorten the duration of fever, reduce or eliminate the need for medications, and enhance the general well-being of patients[19].

The Gate Theory

In my seminars, I reinforce my belief that our purpose as therapists is *not to treat pain*, but to treat unhealthy tissue. If pain were all we cared about, we would ignore the person with quadriplegia who is bleeding from a wound on his leg but

[17] Kiecolt-Glaser, J. K., & Glaser, R. (1992). Psychoneuroimmunology: Can psychological interventions modulate immunity? Journal of Consulting and Clinical Psychology. 60. 569-575.

[18] Chacin-Fernández, J., Chacin Fuenmayor, M., Piñerua-Shuhaibar, L., & Suarez-Roca, H. (2019). Psychological intervention based on psychoneuroimmunology improves clinical evolution, quality of life, and immunity of children with leukemia: A preliminary study. Health Psychology Open. https://doi.org/10.1177/2055102919838902

[19] Schakel L, Veldhuijzen D, S, Crompvoets P, I, Bosch J, A, Cohen S, van Middendorp H, Joosten S, A, Ottenhoff T, H, M, Visser L, G, Evers A, W, M: Effectiveness of Stress-Reducing Interventions on the Response to Challenges to the Immune System: A Meta-Analytic Review. Psychother Psychosom 2019;88:274-286. doi: 10.1159/000501645

doesn't feel a thing. Pain is nothing more than an indicator that something isn't right and must be addressed. The sensations from the pain itself will always be in flux.

People have an organic elasticity to their *pain threshold*, affecting how much they can handle. It's more of a changing barometer than a consistent level. Much like a woman who has begun her labor contractions, each level of pain she reaches ends up resetting what she had previously believed to be the most she could tolerate. Like pain, the way stress impacts us fluctuates as we move through our lives.

Once while clearing blackberries from my front yard, I had a visit from my friend, Gary. I was covered in dirt and garden debris and fully soaked from the sweat dripping down my face.

"Dude," Gary said, looking at my left arm. "You cut yourself. You're bleeding."

I glanced down at my arm, and sure enough, there was a long scratch running from my wrist to my elbow, and the dried blood surrounding it told me it had been there for a while. Suddenly I began to feel the pain from the blackberry thorns—pain which I had not felt until then. My mind had been busy. I had been feeling the sun on my face and the strain of my muscles working. I was enjoying the music in my earphones and the refreshing cold of my bottle of ice water. I had not felt that nine-inch gash on my forearm. Why? Because other sensory input kept my brain busy, drawing attention away from my arm. In the injury treatment world, we refer to this phenomenon as the *Gate Theory*, or the *Gate Control Theory*, because of the invisible 'gates' that keep the pain out when you're distracted with other things.

How does this apply to adversity? When we stop focusing

on the obvious negative impacts of our experiences and instead focus on what's good, what's important, and all the small blessings, whatever they are, the negatives pale and begin to blend into the background.

I have dozens of things I can get into and distract myself— a good movie, a great book, a close game, and the list goes on— but when I focus on my pain, can you guess what I feel? Pain.

Life is like that. When we focus on the negatives, the things we cannot control, like pain, past hurts, what we don't have, how others have wronged us—another long list—then those are the things we feel. We feel the emotional scratches from *the blackberry vines of life!*

I encourage you to focus on what is important, using the *Gate Theory* and filling your mind with thoughts that are good and positive and healthy—the silver linings if you will. Let those things make you smile, and leave no room for that which would rob you of your joy. Continually search for the blessings amidst the pain.

Placebo

Another method that has shown that our beliefs can impact our physiology is the use of *placebo*. As we know, for any prescription medication to be made available to the public, pharmaceutical companies must conduct vast drug studies to determine whether or not the medication is safe and effective. They typically separate study participants into three groups: (1) an *experimental group*, receiving the actual medication, (2) a *placebo group*, receiving a dummy-pill which is inert and contains no active ingredients, and (3) a *control group*, which receives no medication at all. Participants—and often the researchers as well—do not know who is taking the trial medication and who is taking the placebo. Great care is taken to protect the integrity of the studies and prevent individual attitudes and beliefs from skewing the outcome[20] with distorted results. Why? Because the researchers know that believing in something can make it work for you, and believing something works can significantly enhance your brain's response to it.

In fact, the capacity of a placebo to produce such stunning results has given way to a renaissance of sorts in recent years, where researchers are conducting studies on placebos themselves. The results are intriguing to say the least: Larger pills are often more effective than smaller pills, placebo injections can be more effective than pills, and placebo surgeries often produce the most significant effects of all[21].

Other studies have shown that study participants who had a reduction in pain while receiving a placebo continued to have relief after the completion of the study by continuing to take the placebo, even if they *knew* they weren't taking any real medication.

Another intriguing aspect of placebo is known as *nocebo*[22]. When drug study participants begin the study, they're given a complete list of potential side effects the drug is known for. Nocebo refers to the participant believing that a side effect—good or bad—is manifesting when it is not. The studies have

[20] Chen, P.A., Cheong, J.H., Jolly, E. et al. Socially transmitted placebo effects. Nat Hum Behav (2019) doi:10.1038/s41562-019-0749-5

[21] Vedantam, S. (Host). (2019, April 29). All the World's A Stage—Including the Doctor's Office [Audio podcast]. The Hidden Brain. Retrieved from https://www.npr.org/transcripts/718227789

[22] Howick, J., Webster, R., Kirby, N. *et al.* Rapid overview of systematic reviews of nocebo effects reported by patients taking placebos in clinical trials. *Trials* 19, 674 (2018) doi:10.1186/s13063-018-3042-4

shown that a participant's physiology can actually react with false symptoms because he or she is convinced they are experiencing side effects.

Once again, we see that we have the ability to affect our *quality* of life with what we *believe* to be true.

The Power of Choice

The fact that we all haven't experienced the same trials doesn't mean we can't ready and equip ourselves to handle whatever lies ahead. Even if you face wave after wave of adversity as it pounds you relentlessly, you can develop the tools to get through your own trials when they come. They *will* come. *No one* gets a free ride.

Although there were several tools I had in my toolbox while I was dealing with cancer, there was one I had to use before any of the other tools would work. Are you ready for the secret of how I got through?

I chose to.

Your ability to get through anything usually comes down to a choice. *Your choice.* Even giving someone else the power to choose for you is a choice. Each day you make thousands of choices, such as the time you set your alarm to wake you up and how you will spend the day. More importantly, you choose how you respond to difficult events or negative statements made to you by others. It has been said that "between stimulus and response, there is a space. In that space lies our freedom and our power to choose our response. In our response lies our growth and our happiness[23]." You get to choose how you will respond to adversity in your actions and attitude. Remember that if you don't respond at all, your avoidance is a choice as well.

Keeping Your Mind—and Your Eyes—Open

There's something else that can enhance your positive outcomes and help you overcome adversity in your life, and that is being able to recognize helpful messages and solutions as they emerge and appear before you. To explain this, I'm going to tell you a little joke which perfectly illustrates expecting a miracle but not recognizing when it's right in front of you.

A flood is slowly building in the community nearby a woman's home, and a state policeman comes and informs the woman, "Ma'am, a flood is coming. If you come with me now, I can drive you to safety."

"No, but thank you!" she answers. "God is going to save me."

Now fully surrounding the woman's home, the water line continues to rise, forcing her to move to a bedroom upstairs. A volunteer in a rescue pontoon boat approaches her as she stands looking out her second-story window. The volunteer says, "Ma'am, please, climb into the boat. I will take you to safety."

"No," she says again. "God is going to save me."

As the waters rise, the woman climbs up and onto her roof, where she is spotted by a helicopter search and rescue team. The helicopter hovers over the house, and the team begins to

---

[23] Similar variations of this quote have been attributed to numerous authors. https://quoteinvestigator.com/2018/02/18/response

lower a rescue basket. The woman hears the pilot yelling, "GET IN THE BASKET! WE WILL FLY YOU TO SAFETY!"

"No. I'm okay! " she yells back, adamantly. "God is going to save me!!"

The waters continue to rise and the woman eventually drowns. She finds herself entering the gates of heaven. She walks up to God and asks, "God! Why didn't you save me?"

God replies, "Are you serious? I sent a state policeman, a rescue boat, *and* a helicopter! You were expecting something more?"

We turn to our family and friends to help us through the trials of life, yet we're often so full of pride that we won't let them in when they offer the help we need. A friend once told me, "When you deny someone the ability to bless you, you are robbing them of their blessing." What am I saying? GET INTO THE BASKET! Be open to it! I can't promise you that climbing in won't be difficult or leave you with a few scrapes and bumps, but it also might take you to where you need to go!

The Importance of Sleep

Through any kind of healing process, you need to sleep if you hope to emerge stronger. If you aren't getting the sleep you need, you might need to take a self-survey to determine why. It can be due to stress, anger, anxiety, or even to what you are putting into your body to try to "feel better," such as comfort foods, drugs, or alcohol. Let me tell you why sleep is important.

Sleep deprivation has been shown to cause mental health issues, including mood swings, impulsive behavior, anxiety, depression, paranoia, suicidal thoughts, and hallucinations. It can also affect the immune system and create chronic medical conditions such as diabetes and heart disease. Indeed, a lack of sleep can negatively impact *all* of our systems, including respiratory (lungs), cardiovascular (heart and blood pressure), digestive (processing food to provide nourishment to the body), and endocrine (production of hormones.)

Quality sleep has to be a priority in order for you to recover, both mentally *and* physically. You may require a sleep study to determine why you can't sleep or whether you have sleep apnea, a condition that deprives your body and brain of sufficient oxygen while you sleep each night. I ended up wearing one of those uncomfortable—and downright sexy—CPAP masks for a few years following my treatment. I hated it, but it gave me the oxygen I needed to be healthy and to sleep well until my airway was able to function without it.

Choosing to Face Your Struggle

One summer when I was a kid, my mom asked me to spend a few hours straightening up our garage. Soon after I got to work, I squatted down and lifted a heavy box full of family keepsakes. When I started to stand up and turn around, a ladder that had been leaning against the other boxes fell towards me, and the sharp metal at the top rung punctured me in the shoulder. At the same time, the boxes fell on top of the ladder, pressing it deeper into my shoulder. I didn't want to drop what I was holding, so I started to take a step away from the ladder, only to have the sharp metal drag down my back, tearing more deeply into my skin. Now, I had only one option remaining: Drop the box and deal with the ladder.

That's like life. Sometimes you need to drop what you are holding on to and face a problem head-on. Otherwise, it will just dig deeper, causing more pain and leaving bigger scars. When you face your adversity with purpose and intention, accept it for what it is—good or bad—and take action. You will soon be on the path to becoming stronger and more resilient.

CHAPTER NINE
Defense Mechanisms and Coping Strategies

Strength and Resilience

Imagine a plume of tall grass rising from a sandy bluff along the ocean shore. As the intermittent gusts of ocean breezes bombard the long blades of grass, they will bend and dance, acquiescing to the unrelenting assault from the wind. However, if the grass were stiff and unyielding to the invisible torment, it would be more likely to break off and less likely to endure. Do you remember the trees I encountered on my Oregon trail hike? They, too, were flattened because they were unyielding.

We can either try to push back against a situation we have no control over, or we can let go, allow it to flow on past and not try to stop its inevitable journey forward.

In the study of human physiology, we have come to understand that our muscle fibers are either on or off, but never partially engaged. That means our muscles don't have a variable *strength dial* to increase force gradually, so they have to enlist *more* fibers when we need more strength. With that in mind, when I help a patient increase the range of motion of a muscle, one of the methods I use to coax the muscle into relaxing is called Proprioceptive Neuromuscular Facilitation or PNF. I could make it sound complicated, but the technique essentially takes advantage of neurological responses related to breathing and muscle engagement. This is cool—*stay with me!*

Do a quick experiment on yourself: Try to relax your neck and torso while you *simultaneously* take in a deep, lung-filling breath. Did you try it? If you did, you can see it's hard to relax while actively working to fill your lungs. The technique is simple . . . I take the person's limb and move it until it doesn't stretch any further. I hold the limb in place while the person takes a deep breath in *while* they push against my resistance. I hold it for a few seconds and then have them exhale fully while letting go of their pressure. In that moment, the muscle relaxes and allows me to assist them into an even deeper stretch. *It is in the letting go that we find movement and benefit.*

Finding Strength and Courage

In ancient times, masons would mix horsehair into mortar and straw into bricks to help maintain their strength and durability under stress. Thousands of years later, modern building methods still use the same theory, but rather than using horsehair or straw, concrete contractors now have products specially developed to reinforce the cement. While reinforced concrete might crack a little under pressure, it will resist falling apart. On the other hand, unreinforced concrete can easily crumble under pressure.

Our capacity to avoid being crushed or destroyed by adversity comes from within us, and the combination of our thoughts, beliefs, faith, and desire to survive are the components of our invisible reinforcement.

Strength and courage come from within. As adversity presses against you, your mind and body react, compensate, and provide an opportunity for the stress and pressures to strengthen you, which increases your resilience and produces what others see as courage. In the same way that your muscles are made stronger by stress and strain, your heart, mind, and resolve can be strengthened also.

Having courage isn't just about strength alone. It's more of a finished product resulting from the combination of strength, determination, perseverance, perspective, and actively taking our thought processes captive, directing them by conscious choice.

When firefighters purposely enter a building engulfed in flames, they aren't acting out of impulse like a moth to a flame, but as human beings who set aside their fears to do something dangerous with purposed determination.

Processing and Coping

Since many of us don't possess the skills to deal with numerous stressors occurring simultaneously, we organize and store each of the issues in mental *compartments.* Doing so lets us deal with one issue at a time rather than being overwhelmed by all of the issues at once. We call this *compartmentalization.*

A healthy use of compartmentalization is for temporary storage. It gives us a chance to take a rest before opening and dealing with each compartment one-by-one. It *can* be a good thing for us to shove all of our concerns into individual cubbies in the back of our minds because it can help us to *live in the moment* and enjoy productive lives. Many of us, however, end up living our lives as hoarders of unaddressed issues. We keep shoving the stressors back inside and try not to think about them, hoping they will go away.

My experience has shown that those who compartmentalize their past trauma, refuse to think about it, and are averse to seeking counsel, will end up imploding emotionally, resulting in a multitude of problems. Their meltdowns can destroy their lives and relationships and frequently end up manifesting negative physiological responses, such as hypertension, headaches, skin issues, pain, and so on.

Casey Ward, PsyD, a cognitive behavioral therapist in Washington State, says that by compartmentalizing, we can refocus on what is important. Casey explains, "Being able to focus is a natural gift we all have, but how many of us have the ability to refocus? That is a skill you have to develop and takes practice. It's what I work with a lot of athletes on, and it's what you have to work on if you're dealing with adversity. For example, if I am distracted by what's currently going on in my life, if I'm thinking I don't have any money, or I don't have anything to eat, I'm failing at work, or my parents are getting a divorce, those sources of anxiety can put me in a tailspin where none of my challenges get resolved, and I just want to forget about them all. How do I refocus? Notice the whole picture including the accompanying emotion and let it reside in the background of your mind, but pick the most important issue(s) to start with and bring it to the foreground by addressing it systematically from a place of alert attention--mindfulness if you will. *It takes practice.*"

Our system of "processing" involves a complex fusion of emotions that occur while we are grieving or coping, both of which are part of navigating adversity. We must simultaneously heal emotionally while we guard our sanity in the process, using purposeful tactics to do so.

When negative experiences come, our responses can turn primal, as though they are hard-coded into our subconscious, drawing upon our body's sympathetic nervous system. It's what we refer to as the *fight or flight response.*

Just hearing the wailing of a police siren and seeing its flashing red and blue lights in your rearview mirror can invoke your fight or flight response. When that danger or near-paralyzing fear is activated, you experience a physiological shift that is directed instinctively by your nervous system. You likely remember a time when you've felt it. In that moment, your pupils dilate, and your digestive processes pause. Then, your body starts dumping adrenaline and norepinephrine into your bloodstream, which makes your heart beat faster with increased volume and force. It increases your rate of breathing, cranks-up the conversion of the carbs stored in your fat into an influx of available energy, preparing your muscles for exertion. You are now *combat-ready.*

Two common side-effects can occur when your sympathetic nervous system is activated. First, continued stress can keep it stuck in the *on* position, which doesn't allow for the rest, relaxation, and restoration you need from its counterpart, the parasympathetic nervous system. Second, the mental state of your *combat readiness* can lead to poor choices in how you react to the stresses you are facing. Adrenaline alone can turn your coping mechanisms into a survival response based on instinct rather than a choice formed from thoughtful consideration.

Common to all negative coping techniques is the attempt to numb, hide, evade, or distract ourselves rather than purposely deal with what happened and give ourselves the space to grieve. If we don't take the time to *purposely grieve*, we can end up in a downward spiral of behaviors and emotions we may be oblivious to.

Our responses in situations which conjure extreme emotions can result in negative behaviors, even when the emotions are coming from a positive place. The euphoria seems able to lead intelligent people to make foolish choices, which are less about healing and more about compounding the problem.

I once worked briefly as a program counselor for a national weight-loss chain. It certainly was rewarding to see joy and confidence return to the faces of my clients. As their "new" bodies slowly emerged, their personalities also changed and brought them to a place of confidence each time they looked into the mirror.

Unfortunately for some clients, it also brought on a euphoria which often supplanted their moral codes with poor choices. Several clients confessed they had tossed aside common sense and were acting out with risky behaviors. They often were shocked at themselves as their newfound joy transitioned into pain and self-loathing. Attention and compliments from others about how good they looked only served to feed their need for more attention. For some, what had begun as harmless flirtations at the company water cooler ended in the obliteration of the vows they had made to their spouses.

Coping Mechanisms

Have you ever noticed how members of the same family often share mannerisms or vocabulary words? Not on purpose, but on a subconscious level, we tend to emulate those around us in our behaviors and responses. Families that scream at each other usually do so because one or both of the parents were raised with screaming as the family norm during their formative years, and the communication style is perpetuated from parent to child. The response is a *learned behavior*.

Just as we observe how our parents behave and respond to stress, we also observe their attitudes towards life. In the last chapter we discussed how our thoughts direct our emotions, and our emotions direct our behaviors. Well, if parents are constantly depressed, it is probable that their children will grow up hearing their parents' depressive thoughts. They could then take on those thoughts as their own, leading to more depression.

Observing how our parents and siblings respond to stress begins in early childhood. When those first memories are imprinted in us as children, we tend to imitate and copy their responses. However, if we have interpreted their reactions as negative, we might instead purposely respond *inversely* because we don't want to be like our parents.

When intense emotions seem like a curled up monster of an ocean wave which gathers you up before hurtling you into the rocks, having healthy grieving and coping strategies is imperative. It is my experience that most people don't give much thought about planning for future adversity. We have an escape plan from our home in case we have a fire, and we make sure we have a spare tire and jack in the trunk of our car in case we get a flat. Likewise, having a go-to list of coping strategies for dealing with life's stressful events and situations is important and will help bring you increasingly into a healthier state of mental health.

Extreme adversity can be as debilitating as a bomb exploding right in front of you, leaving all of what was once "normal" in scattered ruins amidst the falling debris. You may have once looked into the face of someone who's just experienced something horrific. Their eyes were unfocused as they walked around in a mental stupor, unable to even form a sentence. If that individual had a plan of action in place, it would tend to reduce the likelihood of mental and emotional paralysis when his or her worst fears were realized.

The psychological treatment community has cataloged hundreds of methods people use when coping with extreme stress, either consciously or subconsciously. These coping mechanisms typically fall into one or more coping types, including:

- **Adaptive strategies**, in which individuals tolerate their emotions and stress and choose to make changes in their lives or ways of thinking to more easily adapt to the situation.

- **Avoidance responses**, in which someone chooses to avoid an issue using denial, dissociation, or just not thinking about it.

- **Attacking strategies**, in which the person blames or focuses on others who are often not even involved in the situation.

- **Behavioral responses**, in which someone purposely alters their actions.

- **Cognitive strategies**, in which the person intentionally chooses to change how they think about a stressor.

- **Conversion responses**, when negative thoughts are converted into physical symptoms such as headaches, extreme fatigue, or an ulcer.

- **De-escalation**, such as when you focus on calming yourself down or you have someone else soothe and calm you.

- **Self-harm responses**, in a metaphorical attempt to externally vent out their inner pain or to overcome the numbness which overwhelms their consciousness.

It's helpful to be aware of these common coping mechanisms which you may have previously used in your own life or may have observed being used by others. You have a *choice* in how you react to the emotions you feel from your own adversity. Those in your nucleus of friends, family, and co-workers have choices, too. Your words of encouragement, wisdom, and support can *lead* them to a place of making healthier choices for themselves, but they must make that choice on their own.

It's a good exercise to ask yourself if you have strategies for coping and grieving. I would encourage you to go and grab a pen and paper and brainstorm a list of different things you could do under stressful circumstances to help you regain focus and emerge positively. Your options can include some or all of the following:

- **Creativity**, such as using your hands to paint or making pottery
- **Movement**, such as walking around a lake or going to the nearest bowling alley
- **Relaxation**, such as reading a new book, planting flowers, or getting a massage
- **Engagement**, such as participating in activities with others

The Suicide Option: Ending it All

When the flames and embers of adversity are swirling and your emotional anguish seems insurmountable, attempts to find clarity and perspective can be difficult. That is when some people, for lack of a better solution, think about ending their lives.

Regardless of your religious beliefs about ending your life, the basic idea may find its way into your thoughts at some point in your life. While you might momentarily *think* about suicide (and how sad and sorry others will be when they hear of your demise), you know enough and you possess enough impulse control to ignore the fleeting thought, move on, and put your mind to better use.

When you can't seem to ignore the thoughts and the pain you are feeling seems unbearable, talk to someone! Do your friends, family, and *yourself* a favor and call someone for help. Asking for help does not mean you are weak. Ending your life might seem easy, while confessing your need for help may seem like the hardest thing of all. More people than we realize would be willing to listen to our stories and stand with us to help shoulder our burdens. If you don't have anyone to call, call the Crisis Hotline at 1-800-784-2433. A volunteer will answer your call, someone who wants to be there to talk when you're ready because they want to give back—someone who themselves may have felt similar pain in the past and is now trained and equipped with tools they can share with you.

Getting through the darkest of times can be easier if you give yourself a few moments to take an inventory of the times in your life when you thought *it couldn't get any worse* and later realized there was a positive outcome from your experience. Hold on to those moments. Be thankful. Don't let your current situation block your ability to see the amazing blessings you have had and do have, even the smallest of things. Don't waste time thinking about the things you don't have. You still have air to breathe. You woke up on the right side of the lawn today... giving you another day to be a blessing in the life of another.

When someone you know is entertaining thoughts of suicide, they might exhibit one or more of the following behaviors:

- They make statements about wishing they were never born, or how the world would be a better place without them in it
- They talk, write about, or make jokes about suicide
- They withdraw from their friends or normal activities
- They begin giving away their treasured possessions
- They begin looking for a way to kill themselves, such as a medication or a weapon
- They make statements about or allude to a final goodbye

If this is happening, assume you are the only one who is reaching out. Don't be afraid to ask bluntly if the person is considering suicide. Not only will your inquiry tell them that you care about them and they aren't alone, it will also engage them and get them talking. Ask some key questions, such as:

- You seem down. What's going on? Are you getting help?
- Have you been feeling hopeless about the future?
- Have you been thinking about hurting yourself?

If you believe someone is thinking about suicide, The American Foundation for Suicide Prevention[24] offers this advice:

---

[24] American Foundation for Suicide Prevention. (2020). When Someone Is at Risk. Retrieved March 18, 2020 from. https://afsp.org/find-support/when-someone-is-at-risk

Have an honest conversation ...

- Talk to them in private
- Listen to their story
- Tell them you care about them
- Ask directly if they are thinking about suicide
- Encourage them to seek treatment or to contact their doctor or therapist
- Avoid debating the value of life, minimizing their problems, or giving advice

If a person says they are considering suicide ...

- Take them seriously
- Stay with them
- Help them remove lethal or dangerous means
- Call the National Suicide Prevention Lifeline: 1-800-273-8255
- Text TALK to 741741 to contact a trained crisis counselor from the Crisis Text Line for free, 24/7
- Escort them to mental health services or an emergency room

On a final note, it's important to keep in mind that sometimes without realizing it, you can have a lasting impact on others by your words and actions. You may say something that you think is incidental, while for someone else, it can be truly meaningful—especially if that person is considering suicide. In such a situation, a well-timed word of compassion or encouragement can be monumental and life-changing.

CHAPTER TEN
Purposeful Grieving

All loss carries some level of grieving along with it. Grieving is an essential and necessary component of the healing process. While everyone experiences some kind of loss and grief in their lifetimes, we all grieve somewhat differently regardless of gender, background, age, or culture.

Whether it is the loss of a beloved parent, spouse, pet, friendship, job, or way of life, grieving is natural and should be both anticipated and accommodated. If we hope to ultimately return to a state of emotional health and well-being after going through this experience, we must include purposeful grieving as a part of our process as it is a critical component of healthy coping and helps to build up our resilience in the event of further adversity in the future.

Purposeful grieving in response to a loss requires a decision to turn towards our grief rather than avoid the process. We need to set aside time to reflect and contemplate, and to ask ourselves for honest answers to important questions:

- What have I learned from what I have experienced?
- What or whom do I need to forgive?
- What do I need to let go of that I am still holding on to tightly?
- Am I feeling a sense of guilt?
- Do I feel like a victim?
- Do I feel I'm being punished for something?
- How can I talk about my feelings? In writing? To a friend? If so, to whom?

On the passing of a spouse or child, grief responses can have a wide range. I knew someone who turned a bedroom into a shrine, complete with photos, trinkets, clothing, letters, awards, and more. The room was not to be entered or disturbed by anyone out of respect for the memory of the deceased. At the opposite extreme, I am also familiar with a case in which a surviving spouse quickly boxed up every article of clothing, piece of jewelry, and memento to be stored in the attic. Neither of these responses is necessarily better or more healthy if they are preceded by purposeful grieving.

Purposeful grieving of a child or family member requires setting aside time to fully remember, reminisce, mourn, and celebrate the individual who has passed. That time can be used to purposely embrace one's memories by playing their favorite movie or music, grasping their favorite shirt in your hands and taking in their scent as you hold it close, looking through photos of them, watching videos of you both together, or visiting a place that holds warm memories. Don't be afraid to involve others in your process and have close friends or family join you in purposely grieving your shared loss.

During the interviews I conducted with parents who had lost a child, I had the opportunity to speak with a local fellow named Stormy. He and his wife had lost their underage daughter just two years earlier when she and her 25-year-old boyfriend took their lives together in a Romeo and Juliet type of scenario. They had been seeing each other secretly until the family tried to break them apart. The two decided if they couldn't be together in the present, they would in the next life.

After our interview, Stormy shared some of what he had written in the years since his daughter's death. The following excerpt from his writings will lend some understanding of the pain he still experiences every day as he works through the grief he and his family are still coping with.

> *It is difficult to focus on the living while the deceased play on your mind. I was warned of this early on, and I try my best not to make my kids feel like they have to "compete with their deceased sibling," who, of course, is now only remembered as a sweet angel who must not have done anything wrong - ever. We try to remember only the good things of people who have passed, and surviving children can end up feeling like they have to compete with perfection to measure up. I try to remind my kids that they are still here and can have as much of my attention as they like, but I'm not sure I always have succeeded in that effort.*

I don't feel that old friends have faded away so much as I have faded from them. Not intentionally, but because so many things I used to feel were meaningful or fun have become meaningless. So many things I used to do that were mildly amusing, I no longer find I have the patience for. So many things bore me now, and I would rather just sleep than do them.

Taking a step further, I find myself doing things that I still enjoy somewhat - things I don't have to pay much attention to - things which allow me to essentially turn off most of my thoughts so I can just sit and play. I call it "going mind-numb," but even television doesn't provide an escape like it used to.

I do not take offense to anything people say to me about my loss. I realize that they are trying to contemplate something that is beyond their comprehension. All they want to do is help, but other survivors have told me they get offended, especially over the comments like "It must have been part of God's plan" or "At least something good came of this." But, some are thinking, "How can you think that my child's passing was good?!" I know everyone who says things like this mean well and are only trying to help.

To those of us who are religious - we have probably already used 'God's Plan' as a justification to ourselves, but for it to come from another parent, it could feel like the person is cheering against them. One of the most helpful things in getting through this ordeal is for me to look for that little speck of good that may come out of it, such as a charitable donation, a learning opportunity, or even organ donation. Ultimately, we would trade all of the good which could come from it in a heartbeat in exchange for getting our child back.

CHAPTER ELEVEN
Emerging from Adversity

Asking someone what they hope their future will look like after surviving adversity won't always result in a clear answer. In fact, depending on the intensity of their experience, they might be unable to answer that question at all.

When their storm of adversity has passed, is it happiness they are yearning for? A desire to never feel sadness or pain ever again? Are their goals the same after their hardship or have their previous priorities changed? It's possible their earlier goals no longer hold any importance for them. Perhaps the better question for someone who is currently experiencing extreme adversity is, what is your reason to live?

In 1940, Dr. Viktor Frankl, a distinguished psychiatrist, became the director of the Neurological Department of the Rothschild Hospital, a clinic for Jewish patients. He obtained an immigration visa to emigrate to America but never used it, deciding instead to remain behind and attend to his aging parents.

The following year, Dr. Frankl married Tilly Grosser, a woman he met while living in Vienna. The two were among the last of the Viennese Jews the Nazis allowed to marry but were prohibited from bearing any children. When Tilly became pregnant a short time later, Nazis forced her to abort the baby[25].

In September of 1942 Dr. Viktor Frankl, his wife, and his elderly parents were arrested, herded into train cars, and taken to a Nazi concentration camp where they were immediately separated and stripped of everything they had in their possession, including a manuscript of a book Frankl had been writing. In four different concentration camps over a three-year period, Frankl endured beatings, torture, starvation, sickness, hard labor, and inhumane treatment at the hands of the guards.

Despite the millions murdered in the Auschwitz concentration camp alone, Frankl was one of only 1,200 still alive when the Americans liberated the camp in 1945. After being set free, he learned that every one of his immediate family members had died at the hands of the Nazis except his sister, who had escaped to Australia before later being arrested.

A year after he was liberated, Frankl systematically reconstructed his book manuscript, eventually publishing *Man's Search for Meaning*[26]. The central theme of the book is that *"...everything can be taken from a man but one thing: the last of the human freedoms—to choose one's attitude in any given*

[25] Viktor Frankl Institut. (2019). Viktor Emil Frankl. Retrieved December 17, 2019, from https://www.viktorfrankl.org/biography.html
[26] Frankl, V. E., (1959) Man's Search for Meaning, Boston, Massachusetts: Beacon Press

set of circumstances." While Dr. Frankl could not control the variables of his adversity, he could control the choices he made and how he responded to adversity.

Following significant adversity, most of us emerge changed, and our lives will never be the same. I often hear people say, "I just want things to go back to how they were." I know I've said it, and at some point in life, you might have also. But the likelihood of everything returning to 'normal' following adversity is abysmally low. We don't have a magical remote control that can *rewind our lives* or *undo* a difficult experience. Instead, we must move forward and find our *'new normal.'*

Dr. Frankl couldn't console himself by getting his life back to *normal,* but like that crooked tree along the rocky bluff, he re-engaged with life and began his quest to find what would lie ahead. He was forever changed.

In the last decade alone, hundreds of studies have been published, revealing two major themes common to individuals who had faced adversity. First, in a majority of cases, people who had gone through adverse life events consistently reported better mental health and overall well-being than those who had not. The second was the number of people who had never experienced adversity who viewed their lives as unfulfilling and generally negative. Could it be that adversity can help us emerge better? Stronger? More resilient with a higher level of empathy than we would have had before? I agree with Friedrich Nietzsche who said that weathering the storms of adversity does make us stronger.

Naval Admiral William McRaven, now retired, was the commander of the operation that killed Osama bin Laden. While giving the commencement address at the University of

Texas at Austin in 2014[27], he spoke about the notoriously brutal training of Navy SEAL candidates. The training is so punishing, both emotionally and physically, he said, that eighty percent of the candidates quit before finishing.

As Admiral McRaven explained, "Every day during training, you were challenged with multiple physical events—long runs, long swims, obstacle courses, hours of calisthenics. Something designed to test your mettle. Every event had standards—times you had to meet. If you failed to meet those standards, your name was posted on a list, and at the end of the day, those on the list were invited to a *circus*. A circus was two hours of additional calisthenics designed to wear you down, to break your spirit, to force you to quit. *No one wanted a circus.*"

"A circus meant that for that day, you didn't measure up. A circus meant more fatigue, and more fatigue meant that the following day would be more difficult, and more circuses were likely. But at some time during SEAL training, everyone . . . everyone . . . made the circus list. But an interesting thing happened to those who were constantly on the list. Over time, those students who did two hours of extra calisthenics, got stronger and stronger. The pain of the circuses built inner strength and physical resiliency. Life is filled with circuses."

Indeed, adversity changes us. It can fortify our resilience and strengthen our resolve. The more significant the difficulty, the more opportunity we have for change. It may even prepare us for our new life purpose. How have you been changed by a challenging or adverse experience?

---

[27] McRaven, W. H. (2014, May 19). University of Texas at Austin 2014 Commencement Address - Admiral William H. McRaven [Video file]. Retrieved from https://youtu.be/pxBQLFLei70

A Changed Man; A Changed Life

A year and a half after my major cancer surgery, I received a personal text from my surgeon, Dr. Stephen Bayles, thanking me for the encouraging words on my blog and telling me how reading through my posts had helped him get through a horrific ordeal of his own.

For twenty years, Dr. Stephen Bayles has been a head and neck surgeon, performing complicated procedures that have changed, saved, and extended the lives of thousands of patients. You might assume that working in a profession that regularly confronts people with their own mortality would prepare medical professionals to face their own, but *understanding* isn't nearly the same as *experiencing* it personally.

On a cold winter's morning not long after receiving his text, I met Dr. Bayles at a restaurant adjacent to Virginia Mason Hospital. When we shook hands, the scars on his hand hinted at the frightening story I was about to hear.

Steve had been clearing a section of his property to turn it into pastureland. With all of the brush and debris piled into a large heap, he thought it would be the perfect Fourth of July bonfire for his family. When it came time to light it, he found it difficult to get a fire going, so he doused the pile with gasoline and let it soak in while he went to retrieve a *Roman candle* a friend had given him. When he returned with the firework, he didn't see that the gasoline vapors now surrounded the very spot where he was standing.

"As I lit the Roman candle, I suddenly exploded into twenty-foot tall flames," he recounted to me. "I could feel my lip swelling, and sizzling, and cooking off my face. I could hear the bubbling of my face and felt it swelling. My exposed hands and skin, all the way up to my shoulders, were bubbling and swelling. I dropped immediately to the ground and began rolling around in order to extinguish the flames. As I watched the flames travel across my five acres of dry pasture, I thought about how stupid I was to do what I had done. Just because you have a high IQ doesn't mean you are necessarily smart."

Steve's son ran over and reassured him he was no longer on fire as he helped him to his feet. "I didn't know if I even had ears, a nose, or a mouth, but I immediately felt gratitude that I was still alive! In that moment in time, that was all that mattered. It was kind of a reset moment. I didn't care if I didn't have a nose, a mouth, or ears. It was going to be whatever it was. I was upright and I was alive."

Steve was transported directly to Seattle's Harborview Medical Center Burn Unit where he spent a month recovering from his third-degree burns. "Being there was a complete abdication for me. I was quite vulnerable. I'm used to being the person in charge, taking care of my kids and everything else around me, but now I had to let go of all of that and accept that I didn't have the capacity to do the things I normally do. My greatest fears were losing my career and not being able to provide for my kids in any capacity— emotionally, mentally, or physically. I knew I had to do what the doctors told me and be a good patient, and trust those who were taking care of me, just as I ask my patients to put their trust in me. It was the ultimate exercise in vulnerability and dependency, as I relied on others to get me through it."

He continued, "In my recovery, I constantly reminded myself that people all around me were navigating much more difficult things. I had burns, yet they were healing. My cancer patients overcome and manage much worse situations than what I went through, and they don't always have the happy ending I had. Now I remind myself daily how blessed I am and how many people have it worse, so I don't feel I have the right to complain."

I asked Steve if he had observed any common traits among those of his patients who seem to navigate through adversity successfully. "The patients I see who are successful in their journey come out with a clear sense of gratitude and humility," he said. "They don't tend to dwell on what they've lost, but focus instead on what the experience has done for them.

"Believing in something that is greater and more important than yourself, and recognizing that your life has meaning in its capacity to serve others—in whatever form or fashion—is the purpose of life. It is what's necessary to get through all of this.

"I now have a completely new perspective of what my patients go through. I am a better doctor because of my experience and can offer something that I couldn't offer before. Every roadblock can give you the opportunity for something new, and if you embrace it, you can grow from it.

"When I find myself worrying about the future, I have to catch myself and remember to stay here in the present. I'm not sure who it's from, but there is a quote that has stayed with me through this process, which says, *'If you are depressed you are living in the past. If you are anxious, you are living in the future. If you are at peace, you are living in the present'.*"

Today, Steve is back at work as a surgeon at Virginia Mason

Hospital in Seattle. He is a changed man and is grateful for the journey that led him to healing, enlightenment, and a higher level of understanding.

CHAPTER TWELVE
Fear vs. Fortitude

Reflecting back on all my experiences, I think my biggest fear through it all was telling my three daughters I had cancer. I was more afraid of that than I was of losing my business or my house. I knew my words were going to trigger deep emotions in them and I didn't know if their lives would ever be the same.

At the time, all three of my girls were deeply immersed in their lives and actively involved in different activities with their friends and classmates. Ashley was 20 years old and living on her own across town. Sara was 16 and living abroad as an exchange student. Holly was 13 and going back and forth between her mom's house and mine. They were all doing well holding their own, and I was about to turn their world upside down. How could I tell them that I had cancer, the disease that kills millions of people every year?

They knew what cancer was, of course. But when you learn that this time it's your father who has it, the ground you stand on can suddenly seem to shake and crumble beneath your feet. Dads are supposed to be invincible. Our kids believe we can (and will) fix anything that's broken, beat up any bad guy, and proudly walk them down the aisle on their wedding day. I knew beyond a doubt that if their father died before they were ready (if we're ever really *ready*), it would be a major, life-changing trauma for my three girls.

I had just been informed myself that I had cancer, so I was still trying to process the diagnosis and wrap my head around all its implications. In other words, I was still somewhat of an incoherent, emotional mess. How could I deliver the news in a rational, parental, not-to-worry-we-got-this-under-control voice when I wasn't sure I could even hold my own emotions in check? I so wanted to be strong for them.

I decided I had to sugar-coat the news a little and try to downplay the diagnosis—for all our sakes, even though I knew my girls would see the truth regardless of what my words were saying. After determining how and when to talk with them, I arranged to meet separately with each one, all on the same day. I had to give Sara the news over a Skype video call.

Each of the girls took the news amazingly well. Years later they confessed they all knew the actual situation was more dire than I was letting on, but they wanted to be strong for me. In hindsight, I think it's better to give the whole truth upfront so they can deal with it rather than be potentially devastated later when they realized I'd not been truthful with them and the situation was way worse than I had told them it was.

As a survivor, I've learned that most people who've gone through cancer have an ongoing fear of recurrence, even if they've been in remission for many years. Why wouldn't they? Another nightmarish diagnosis followed by grueling treatment procedures year after year? It's not hard to understand how this could be emotionally paralyzing.

In general, I'm not a very superstitious person. Yet, when it comes to speaking out loud about the possibility of cancer returning to wreak more havoc, I simply do not. It's not because I fear it could happen just because I spoke it into existence or put it out into the universe. It's because worry and angst are the seeds from which illness can grow, and I've decided they aren't a productive use of the precious time I have left. Life's too short.

What we do with the scary thoughts that flood our minds can make the difference between emerging a broken shell of our former selves and emerging stronger and better prepared for the future. If you think about what all of your future possibilities might be instead of what your limitations are, who knows what you can accomplish?

When emerging from adversity, most of us envision a linear path that begins at Position A, a place which would be considered normal, then moves to Position B, representing the tumultuous events of our adversity, and ends at Position C, where we land on the other side of our trouble and take time for our recovery and restoration—but what if we never emerge from Position B and are destined to remain in that reality forever?

By now, you've figured out that I like analogies, so here's another one: Let's compare our adversity to a clothes dryer—an emotional clothes dryer, if you will. Now, think of yourself as a tennis shoe inside, being tossed about in a hot and hostile environment, banging around loudly. What if the dryer door never opens, and you can never escape the unrelenting turmoil? How do you respond to the news your condition will never improve, that this is your new normal, and it may even get worse?

Whether we are facing short-term adversity or will be going through it for a long time to come, we must choose to thrive rather than simply survive. What do we need to be able to make that choice? Fortitude—the strength of mind that allows us to meet and survive adversity with positivity and courage.

As you are about to learn, my friend, Jim, a medic and firefighter, is a perfect example of someone who has—and exercises—fortitude.

I met Jim a year after I finished going through cancer treatment. He and a buddy of mine were working together as medics, and he had been living with Stage 4 lung cancer, so I wanted very much to meet him. With my friend's help, we arranged a meeting at a local coffee shop, just to talk, exchange war stories, and provide mutual encouragement.

Truth be told, I expected to see a shriveled, defeated man who had been dealing with the ravages of cancer. When he walked through the door of the café, however, he was full of life and vitality. He offered me his hand, and with a firm handshake said, "Jim Brown. Nice to meet you."

I asked Jim to tell me about his illness and how it had affected him and his family. As his story unfolded, the brawny firefighter related his experience with incurable cancer with a demeanor that almost felt as though the story was about someone else. Based on some breathing issues Jim had been having, his doctor had run a battery of tests that had ultimately revealed an abnormality in his lungs. He learned he had Stage 4 metastatic lung cancer, which meant it wasn't confined to his lungs alone. The cancer had also made its way into his abdominal cavity and one of his hip bones.

"It turned my world upside down," Jim said, "and it put me into crisis mode that lasted four months."

In his first blog post[28] about his condition, Jim was frank about his mindset. "My disease is being categorized as Stage 4," he wrote. "But stop right there! Don't look up any statistics! They do not apply to me, so don't waste your time!"

As a cancer survivor myself, I know others who have dealt with Stage 4 lung cancer, but none have gone through treatment while at the same time snowboarding and competing in mountain bike races. Jim was refusing to act like his life was about to end. He focused instead on living and had no intention of letting cancer get in his way of being a husband, father, medic, and friend. He felt he didn't have time for self-pity and was determined he wouldn't be leaving this life anytime soon. This cancer was merely a nuisance to Jim, and there was so much left he wanted to do. He was determined to do it, but his official life expectancy wasn't good. The American Cancer Society's website had predicted that Jim would most likely lose his battle within less than five years[29].

---

[28] Brown, J. (2015, May 24). The Lay of the Land. http://thedudeisthedad.blogspot.com/2015/05/the-lay-of-land.html

[29] American Cancer Society. (2019). Lunch cancer survival rates. Retrieved December 16, 2019 from https://www.cancer.org/cancer/lung-cancer/detection-diagnosis-staging/survival-rates.html

When I asked Jim what he considered the toughest part of his cancer experience, he had an answer right away. "Telling my wife and daughters I had cancer was the hardest thing I've ever done in my life," he said.

After meeting Jim that day, three years passed. I wanted to interview him for this book but wasn't even sure if he was still alive. Indeed, he was! In fact, Jim's Facebook page was filled with photos and stories about his recent activities, travel, family life, and so on. I was thrilled when I saw that his most recent update had just been posted that morning. I shot him a quick text and we scheduled a time to meet the following week.

When Jim arrived at the coffee shop, he looked different. He brought me up to date as we sat at the coffee bar. Despite the lengthy series of chemotherapy treatments he had undergone, his cancer had progressed into his lymph nodes. Follow-up scans had revealed the cancer had also metastasized to his brain and into a rib (which had actually broken due to the cancer it contained). That said, he was about to leave for two weeks in Peru with a cancer support and advocacy organization. The group, appropriately called A Fresh Chapter[30], provides opportunities for cancer survivors to be challenged and explore their future possibilities beyond cancer. With a new medication showing promise, Jim's doctors had given him the go-ahead to travel.

What really seemed to be on Jim's mind, though, despite his ongoing medical issues and exciting travel plans, was the enormous, self-imposed pressure of trying to be the man he thought he was supposed to be.

---

[30] https://afreshchapter.com

His first blog post after his return from Peru opened with the simple proclamation, "My trip to Peru changed my life!" His entire experience, together with the many conversations he had had with the other cancer survivors, as well as an important documentary[31] film he had watched while there, had all worked together to heal him emotionally and help him overcome his concerns about his masculinity. He learned it was okay to not be strong all the time, and to be vulnerable.

"All the things that made me who I thought I was were stripped away on this trip," Jim wrote. "I was able to let go and embrace who I am now, and that is someone who inspires people."

When we met again about a month after he had returned from Peru, Jim told me that a recent scan had shown that his brain metastases were gone, his rib was healing, and there was no evidence of the cancer spreading. He also talked about his wife's ongoing strength and how her support had been such a help to him.

"Rather than trying to convince me to spend more time with her and the girls, she's given me the freedom to do whatever I've needed to do and go wherever I've needed to go to find peace and strength. She is very much a rock."

Jim has been changed by his cancer experiences. His emotional healing can best be described as a metamorphosis that's left him a changed man. He is living proof that facing adversity with fortitude gives us more capacity for life.

---

[31] Congdon, J., Newsom, J.S., & Anthony, J. (Producers), & Newsom, J.S. (Director). (2015). The Mask You Live In [Motion Picture]. United States: The Representation Project.

CHAPTER THIRTEEN
A New Normal

Our lives are almost always different somehow in the aftermath of adversity—to some degree or other. The change might be obvious, such as the loss of a life partner, or a new job, or a physical change such as the loss of a limb. On the other hand, it could be a new outlook, a new sense of trust or empathy, or even a new sense of purpose in one's life. How we interpret these changes—whether they have enhanced our lives or hurt them in some way—is up to us. However we perceive these changes in our lives, they are what we refer to as our "new normal."

In the months following my surgery and subsequent treatments, my life continued, but what I knew to be normal did not. I remember one day when I was preparing to leave the hospital to come home (finally!), and one of my doctors—figuring he'd glean some free advice while I was still there—was asking me questions about how to treat his recent back injury. With all the sutures holding my tongue together, I had to speak carefully as I shifted into instructor-mode and explained the benefits of heat when applied to inflamed tissue.

As I spoke, I became increasingly self-aware of the sound of my voice and the way I was pronouncing words. No longer did I have the rich baritone voice I had always had. Instead, my voice was weak and shaky. Even worse was how my speech was now hampered enough that the doctor had great difficulty understanding what I was trying to say. For many months, my mouth had clearly been a 'war zone' and it clearly sounded like it. It took many tries and a lot of patience and humility, but I was finally able to make myself understood. I think.

I also came out of this experience with huge medical bills. I would love to have had the resources to pay them off immediately, yet the opposite was true. I hadn't worked in a very long time and—as a professional seminar speaker—I wasn't going to be back in front of an audience any time soon. That's the thing about public speaking: You have to be able to speak and be understood. I hoped the financial office at the hospital would be flexible and show some empathy toward my bleak situation. My life had suddenly become one in which I would have to practice considerable restraint when it came to spending money.

In addition, there were myriad changes in my day-to-day mobility, well-being, and self-care as a result of my surgeries. I was now choking on food and water because of changes in the structure of my mouth. I had mild tingling in my spine, intense pins-and-needles in my neck, and spasms in my legs and feet.

I had occasional difficulty catching my breath, blood-flow issues in my hands, and a very limited sense of taste and smell. (I accidentally lit my bathrobe on fire while making breakfast last week.)

That doesn't even include the many side effects of chemo and radiation.

I could now eat only soft, non-spicy foods. After a meal, I had to excuse myself to the restroom so I could cough, hack, and dislodge the food which remained stuck in the altered physiology of my mouth and throat.

If all that wasn't enough, I started experiencing a kind of fog—a noticeably impaired memory—that is affectionately referred to by cancer survivors as chemo brain. Yes, it's a real thing, and to this day, I am impacted by it. Everyone who knows me well can see it.

This, my friends, has all become my *new normal*. Back then, it was a lot to adjust to, and it took me a long time to accept these changes. Today, more than six years after my surgery and follow-up treatments, I have successfully adapted to most of these new rules and restrictions. However, at the time, it seemed that would never happen.

Hoping your post-adversity life will be the same as it was before is a futile exercise. The truth is that nothing can or will ever be the same as it was. Life changes. The world changes. People and places change, too. We definitely change and transform following our experiences with adversity. There is no going back. Our realities from before will never be the same as after. The good news is, we have a choice regarding how that transformation process develops.

So, how did I do it? First and foremost, I had to learn to anticipate what was going to be different and plan accordingly. I sought speech therapy so I could re-learn how to speak in a way people would understand me. I had to slow down, pick my words carefully, become intentional in enunciating, and develop more patience with myself and others who needed me to repeat what I had said—sometimes several times!

Before surgery and cancer, I was a big fan of eating out. Enjoying a glass of wine, a thick steak, and a decadent dessert with friends was how I rewarded myself for a hard day of work. With all that is different, I've had to make adjustments on that front. Now, when someone suggests we stop by a neighborhood eating establishment, I usually respond by saying, "How 'bout we go grab coffee or a beer?"

Eating out less often has had benefits too, of course. I eat less, and I'm more conscious of healthy choices when it's me who's doing the grocery shopping and food prep. Mostly, it has kept my credit card safely inside my wallet and vastly reduced my monthly spending.

When I see a new book or a shiny new toy, it takes me an extra second to remember I'm still not in the position to acquire whatever I want. Those days may come, but my whole attitude about new acquisitions has changed anyway. I'm still glad just to be waking up in the morning; I can probably live without a new sports car.

Being honest, writing this chapter about all the negative side effects my cancer treatment goes against the grain of who I am—or at least, who I've become. Dwelling on what's different, or what I now don't have, or what could have been, suddenly seems like a ridiculous waste of time. I mean, what is the point?

In truth, things could have been much worse. For one thing, without treatment for my cancer, I would be dead, so there's that. I certainly wouldn't need a new kayak in that case. The surgery didn't have to be successful. They could have misdiagnosed my condition and taken out the wrong thing. They could have made it so that I would never speak again. They could have dropped the scalpel and sliced up my face. All kinds of things could have gone wrong. But they didn't.

Focusing on the negative won't change things for the better, and complaining about my new normal doesn't make for very interesting conversation. Being alive in exchange for some enduring discomfort or minor deprivation seems like a fair trade. Even with all the negative outcomes and side effects from treatment, I can tell you the single most significant upside for me is that I am alive.

Besides, reminding myself of the *things I do have,* and *what I can do,* is a better use of my time than complaining about the things I can't. I can kayak in our lake, bicycle through the countryside, hike the numerous trails in our area, travel with my wife, and pursue my joy of photography. Thankfully, I now have the stamina and the ability to speak clearly enough to present seminars for up to eight hours a day. I'm back to making a living, doing what I enjoy and most want to do.

Do I have reason to complain about what I don't have and can't do? Sure, but focusing on all the positives in my life brings me a lot more joy.

A Shared New Normal

It is spring of 2020, and as this book is being prepared for publishing, we are dealing with a global pandemic that has sent nearly every country into concurrent medical, financial, and social tailspins. As we know, in late 2019, out of Wuhan, China, a new or *novel* coronavirus began infecting people. Because the associated illness, named Covid-19, is new, there is no vaccine or cure for it. Before a vaccine is developed and ready for use, the virus will remain extremely deadly and may potentially result in a higher death rate than the Spanish Flu pandemic that occurred in 1918.

When the pandemic hit, the United States—like most other countries—was not prepared, despite numerous experts warning us of the possibility of this happening. As a result, hospitals have been strained by overcrowding and a disturbing shortage of equipment. Health workers and others on the front lines have been risking their lives to care for their patients, and many have succumbed to the virus as well. Businesses large and small have been forced to temporarily close their doors in hopes of reducing the occurrence of the infection. We expect many of them to never reopen. Our country is seeing the highest numbers of unemployment claims since the Great Depression[32] in the early twentieth century. From a social standpoint, Americans have essentially been told to shelter in place, i.e., "stay home and stay safe." The pandemic is affecting everyone and everything, and we will likely see its impact rippling across the globe for years to come.

---

[32] Soergel, A. (2020, May 8). Unemployment highest since great depression as coronavirus collapses labor market. U.S. News & World Report. Retrieved from https://www.usnews.com/news/national-news/articles/2020-05-08/unemployment-highest-since-great-depression-as-coronavirus-collapses-labor-market

Writing this feels surreal in a way; it is like being blindfolded but still expected to move forward without knowing whether the ground will still be there to meet our next steps. While our shared past has allowed us to assume the future will be pretty much the same as it has been and our future normal will closely resemble what our lives have been like in the past (or even better), we can see now that that may not be the case at all, and no one can promise us that any longer.

Our nation's collective new normal is still to be determined, and every decision our leaders make today will affect tomorrow's new normal. We have no guarantees as to what tomorrow will look like, except the guarantee that life will change. Your future direction may not be what you had planned.

Earlier in this book, I compared adversity to blades of grass being blown by the ocean wind. The grass survives, not because it wants to stay the same but because it has no expectation of what direction the wind might come from next, or how hard and for how long it will blow. Being flexible and willing to accept the certainty of uncertainty is the best way for us to find peace about what tomorrow will bring.

CHAPTER FOURTEEN
The Support Network

When you are going through the ups and downs of life, the last thing you want is to navigate it alone. Rather than marooning yourself in isolation and believing you can handle it all alone, it's important to accept the help and support of those who want to be there for you. Revealing your struggle rather than showing a stiff upper lip is a sign of strength and maturity—*not* a sign of weakness.

I read a study recently regarding social support and how it affects our life expectancy. I was stunned to learn that the positive effects of social support can be *equally as powerful* as the negative effects of smoking cigarettes. Potentially, your support network can literally be the difference between life and death, and accepting their help and support can be imperative to your recovery and getting your life back. Regardless of how strong you think you are, you don't need to go through adversity alone.

Numerous other studies have shown that navigating a challenging time in your life with the help of a support network usually produces positive effects on us both physically and mentally. In addition, we have learned that the *quality* of that time spent with those in our support network is more important than the *quantity* of time[33]. Studies also have shown how social support networks can help break the cycle of adversity for children[34] who are or have been raised in homes with high levels of parental stress and dysfunction.

Generally speaking, a support network, or support system, is a group made up of individual people who work together to provide practical, physical, emotional, and moral support when a family or individual are having difficulties accomplishing everyday issues. Support networks are typically made up of friends, family members, and/or co-workers. The people in a support network may or may not know one another, but they do know the individual or family they are collectively supporting.

Ideally, for the sake of our health and safety, we should all have a network of people we can count on to have our backs when life doesn't go as planned. For example, after enduring an automobile accident, if we find ourselves at home for respite and recovery, having a support network in place can ensure there is food in the house, we have transportation to and from medical appointments, the dog is being walked, and someone

[33] Teo AR, Choi H, Valenstein M (2013) Social Relationships and Depression: Ten-Year Follow-Up from a Nationally Representative Study. PLoS ONE 8(4): e62396. https://doi.org/10.1371/journal.pone.0062396
[34] http://www.urbanchildinstitute.org/articles/features/social-support-can-help-break-the-cycle-of-adversity

is taking care of everything else necessary for a smooth period of recuperation. It's a lot fewer things we need to worry about when we already have a lot on our minds.

Some support networks are fairly informal and organic while others are more organized and coordinated. Some start small, but in time add more people if the need is there. If the members of a support network are not able to meet all the needs of an individual receiving support or if they determine that more formalized support should be accessed, they can broaden the network of support to include a church group, perhaps, or a group like AA, or a hospital-based support program, in which there may be more accountability and coordination of purpose.

When Is a Support Network Needed?

How do we know when we need a support network? Will *we* recognize when we do, or will our friends and family members realize it and make it happen?

Following a period of adversity, some people will do just fine on their own, while some will need just a little help and others may need full-time assistance. Another variable might be the length of time the support network remains active. If you've just learned that your company is going out of business and you're out of a job, you may need your support network to step up for a few days or a week or two, to be sure you're coping with the news, you've got the necessary financial reserves in place to survive, you're not getting depressed, and your resume has been updated so you can start sending it to prospective employers.

In a very different scenario, if your house burns down and you lose everything. It is likely you will need more comprehensive support for several months, starting with friends to feed you dinner and give you a temporary place to sleep, to finding a long-term place to live, the use of essentials until you're able to replace them yourself, and obtaining copies of important documents you've lost in the fire. In that case, along with friends and family members, there are usually local support organizations and neighborhood associations that can provide additional support, resources, and hands-on help.

Organizing the Support Network

Every support team comes together somewhat differently, ranging from casually taking turns dropping by to having someone in charge putting a purposeful plan in place. Once your support services have begun, remember that good communication is imperative for providing appropriate support services, reducing duplication of efforts, and ensuring that the support lasts as long as it is needed.

Today, social media platforms and care-focused websites can be invaluable in facilitating team communication and planning. For example, the support team can set up a private social media group or group page on sites such as Facebook, Google, or similar. Video conferencing can be used for regularly-scheduled video chats to help everyone stay updated and informed. When the situation calls for it, you can even create a *how-to* video demonstrating specific routines or methods used in providing support.

Just Do It

Even if an official support team isn't in place, you can always make a positive difference by just helping someone in need. Your neighbor whose car broke down ... your co-worker whose husband has been deployed ... your friend who broke her leg in a skiing accident ... your sister who suddenly has to take a business trip—all would be endlessly grateful for your help, whatever form it may take.

So, you call your neighbor or co-worker and ask, "What can I do to be helpful?" Surprisingly, they say, "Nothing, really." Why? Because they're struggling with a bit of adversity and aren't necessarily thinking clearly, so they can't spontaneously come up with tasks you can do for them. They also—like the rest of us—don't like asking for help.

Next time, try using a different tactic. If your neighbor's car has broken down, call and tell her when you're leaving for church and invite her to come along. If your co-worker's husband has been deployed and she's alone with four children, buy her a gift card for a local pizzeria. If your friend broke her leg, find her mailbox and bring over her mail. Or, if your sister leaves on a sudden business trip, put her mind at ease by telling her you're taking care of her plants till she returns. The more specific you can be, the less they can object to your offer of assistance.

In the days and weeks following my surgery, I relied on my support network for all my meals, trips to the doctor, and various activities of daily living. When my good friend, Kris, noticed on social media that I had recently had surgery, she sent me a text telling me she was coming over the next day. I was so happy, and looking forward to seeing her and catching up. After hugging me when she first arrived, however, she quickly informed me she was going to clean my house. She wasn't asking for my permission. She wasn't offering some ambiguous, non-specific favor. She wasn't asking how she could help. She just showed up and did what clearly needed to be done.

Don't Filter

There's something else we tend to do when we're trying to be supportive of a friend or—especially—a family member. It's logical to want to protect someone who's contending with the realities of the outside world from bad news or further adversity. *They've got enough to worry about,"* we think. *"The last thing they need is me adding to their problems!"*

During my time in the hospital, it became clear to me that my friends and family had stopped sharing anything about their daily lives or any of their various troublesome issues. *Nothing!* When I quizzed them about it in the months following, several confessed they didn't want to overload me or burden me with their own problems. "You're going through enough already," explained one of my friends.

While I love my friends for caring enough about me to want to protect me, I probably would have liked it better if they had indeed told me about their struggles. For one thing, it would have been a welcome and distracting diversion for me to focus on and get my mind off my own unpleasant situation. Plus, it's nice to know you can still be a good friend to others even when you're laid up with an illness or injury. You're still *you.*

Another Point of View

At one point during my treatment a friend told me that refusing to let someone help or support me was *robbing them of their blessing*. Her words made me pause and reflect. I love to help other people, but I have a difficult time receiving help. My issue is I don't want to be a burden to anyone, so the idea of *accepting* help, let alone *asking* for it, is foreign to me.

My friend Barry had the same perspective, but after losing the use of his legs he realized that it was *asking* for help that has been one of the biggest reasons he has been successful in life. If we can only set aside our fears of looking weak or of being seen at our worst, we will come to realize people *want* to be supportive and *want* to offer help. It's in accepting their blessing that we won't rob them of theirs.

As Barry told me, "Asking for help has opened up the world for me, helping me take on challenges without as much fear." That is the beauty of support networks. In our darkest hour, they will step forward to help us take on life's challenges *without as much fear.*

When Support Becomes Caregiving

When you are part of someone's support network, your role is to provide companionship and assistance wherever or however it's either needed or requested. While doing this can be a blessing to the person receiving support, it can also start to feel like a burden to you, especially if you are fully immersed in your own busy life and career, and the level of support needed is high. When that becomes the case, it is probably time to consider a regular caregiver to take over care responsibilities, or a companion who would essentially be a fellow traveler on the journey.

When your child or spouse are sick or recovering, you don't question your role in providing their care. You're just glad you are there for them. Yet, when it comes to parents, or siblings, or friends, you may feel differently. Depending on your relationship with them, your desire to care for them may not be as automatic. I have seen people suddenly flung into the responsibility of caring for a family member because there was no one else. They had no choice, and there was no other option but to help—whether they wanted the extra responsibility or not. Regardless of whether you purposely choose to help someone or you accept your *de facto* role as caregiver, for the sake of your sanity, it is a good idea to come to terms with what lies ahead and give yourself the grace to take on the responsibility. Taking some time and deciding that *you want to* take on the responsibility as an active choice rather than a passive acceptance, will reduce your likelihood of becoming resentful and seeing the responsibility as a burden.

Unless you are a professional caregiver, volunteering to help a friend or loved one for any extended period of time can lead to its own set of issues. Cobie Whitten, a PhD in clinical psychology and psycho-oncology consultant, says, "We all cope differently, and working through adversity with loved ones who may cope differently than you is like a delicate dance." She adds, "Adversity does not happen in a vacuum – so whatever issues your relationship had prior to the adversity are often still variables in the process."

When I had just returned home from the hospital following

my big surgery, one of my sisters was able to move in with me and be part of my support network. It didn't take long, however, for Lisa's job description to change. As the nausea from my chemotherapy resulted in frequent unpleasant trips to the bathroom, she found herself standing beside me at some of my worst moments. There she'd be, with her hand on my back in a sign of emotional support, even though she had to look away with her eyes tightly closed and face contorted as though she'd just seen fresh roadkill. (I'm sure she would have held my hair back if I had any.) Another time, Lisa set up a cot at the foot of my bed because she was worried I might not wake up. I later learned she got up once an hour to make sure I was still breathing. It couldn't have been fun or easy for her, but still, she chose to be there, and that meant the world to me.

If You Aren't Grounded, You Aren't Helpful

Caregiving can be deeply satisfying, knowing you are making a difference at a critical point in someone's life. Yet it can also be extremely stressful. Caregivers have been known to get so worn out they can no longer provide the care their loved one is counting on.

Remember that we cannot take care of anyone else until we take care of ourselves. If you find yourself in a caregiving role, be sure to take care of *you*. First, write down what you need—the things or activities that you know will help you refresh and renew. Then choose a few and schedule them in your calendar, *preferably in permanent marker*. Next, find someone to talk or vent to—a trustworthy friend, perhaps, or even a mental health professional. Take time for yourself but be sure not to abandon other parts of your life as well; your social interactions can be equally as important as having time alone to decompress and get centered again. If nothing else, go people-watching in the mall or downtown. Take a drive or walk in nature for a change of scenery, a breath of fresh air, and a fresh new perspective if you need it. You must take care of yourself if you hope to be of any use to the person you are caring for!

Create a Care Team Manual

If you are part of a caregiving team, consider creating a care team manual—a go-to resource containing vital information that will help the caregivers provide a good continuity of care. When putting together a manual, include pertinent details, such as (1) all personal information (name, address, age, date of birth, social security number); (2) current medical diagnosis if there is one; (3) contact information for health care providers, other providers, family members and close friends; (4) a list and schedule for all current medications, vitamins, and supplements; (5) all allergies including food and drug allergies; (6) related legal documents, such as a DNR order or a medical power of attorney.

The central component of the care team manual will be the record keeping logs to help monitor consistency of care and the patient's progress. You might include physical activity, moods and emotions, pain levels and frequency, and one's ability to communicate clearly and function independently, Of equal importance is a daily record of food eaten and portion sizes, the caregivers' observations of physical and emotional health concerns, a record of weight loss/gain, and of course, details of medications taken, dosage, frequency, and so on.

It is the responsibility of each member of the caregiving team to update the manual when changes occur. Finally, keep in mind that privacy can be an issue if someone with malintent were to access the manual. Take steps to protect it from unauthorized individuals.

Support for Mom or Dad

A few words about the people in your life who are aging: It is not uncommon for older people to need a support system, whether or not they have been facing a period of obvious adversity in their lives. Aging *is* their adversity. This is especially true if they wish to remain living independently in their own homes. Adult children and neighbors can often provide the support necessary, at least at first, until it becomes obvious that a move to a more supportive environment needs to take place.

Unfortunately, as part of the aging process, your parent, grandparent, or older friend may be struggling with cognitive function issues and might not be aware they are losing the ability to care for themselves. This would reduce the likelihood that they would ever reach out to others and ask for help.

It is helpful to be aware of some specific indicators that *you* can watch out for. For example, if you see that your parent is getting more confused and forgetful than usual, missing appointments, or neglecting to take their medications, it's time to discuss the benefits of a support network. If they are falling with some frequency, finding it difficult to get out of a chair, or having trouble walking, remind them that a support network may extend the time they can live on their own. Certainly, that will also apply to anyone whose activities of daily living may have become questionable. Look around to see if their home is dirtier than usual, laundry or dishes haven't been washed, bills aren't being paid, or their personal hygiene is starting to suffer. Those are the most common warning signs that a support network is needed.

A note of caution: Something almost all older people have in common is their determination to remain self-sufficient and never become a burden on others. Older people are also known for possessing a streak of stubbornness they will reliably demonstrate when their adult children start hinting at taking away their car keys or finding a lovely new retirement community to move into. Please don't feel you have to take on these difficult moments alone. Go together with your siblings or with other members of the support network—and *support each other*. Include a professional when warranted. The library or Internet will have many resources that are specifically intended for families experiencing these life-changing events.

Boundaries

We all know that a boundary is usually some kind of a physical demarcation, such as a fence or wall along a property line that clearly indicates where one person's yard ends and another's begins. "High walls good neighbors make" is an often-heard quote referring to the privacy each neighbor can enjoy behind a well-placed boundary, thus reducing the occurrence of drama and conflict between the two neighbors. While *personal boundaries* aren't something you can see like a wall, they serve essentially the same purpose: providing a set of clearly specified limitations people set for themselves regarding what they *consider to be safe, permissible, and acceptable behaviors of others towards them.*

We usually define our own set of boundaries based on a combination of our past experiences, social observations, attitudes, and personal beliefs. Just as new laws are often the result of negative events, boundaries are often put into place to protect ourselves from certain actions or treatment by others which perhaps made us feel uncomfortable or unsafe.

In the context of support networks, the difference between the individual who's being *supported* and the person who is *providing* the support is the level of control they have over one another. That said, the absence of effective boundaries between and among people can ultimately be as detrimental to the person receiving support as well as to those offering it. If the supporter abuses their role in the situation and acts from a place of power or authority, the supported person can be left feeling helpless, disrespected, or taken advantage of. This is why it is critical to establish personal boundaries in a supportive or caregiving relationship.

Boundaries for the Supported

Everyone knows people who fail to set and observe good boundaries between themselves and others. It is particularly important to maintain personal boundaries when you find yourself in a supportive or caregiving scenario.

To understand what some *healthy boundaries* would be for someone who is being supported, let's first look at examples of what *unhealthy* boundaries might look like:

- You ask the people in your support network to take on more than is reasonable or expected in their role

- You expect others to defer to your rules, preferences, and schedule
- You criticize the way others complete tasks
- You allow or expect others to make decisions for you rather than taking responsibility for your own choices
- You continuously apologize for being in your situation and needing support
- You fail to acknowledge or show gratitude for what others are doing for you
- You disregard societal norms regarding personal privacy, decency, and hygiene

Now, in contrast, here are some *healthy* boundaries:
- You convey clear expectations and needs to those who want to support you
- You respect other people's lives, schedules, families, and financial limitations
- You understand that your needs and preferences may differ from others'
- You acknowledge your right to have your own emotions, feelings
- You don't allow others to disrespect, disregard, or abuse you
- You don't allow others to take their anger and frustrations out on you
- You share information with others when and if you choose to
- You are assertive and stand by your decisions

- You express appropriate levels of appreciation and frequent recognition of the support being provided

There are distinct benefits to taking a self-inventory to clarify to yourself what your needs are to help you feel safe and supported. Once you've defined your boundaries, it is critical that you make them known to others; personal boundaries are useless unless they are clearly communicated. It's a good idea to set aside time for a frank discussion regarding your needs and expectations with members of your network. For some people, it helps to write down their personal boundaries so they can be reviewed and referred to if necessary.

Boundaries for the Supporters

Good boundaries are just as important for those who are supporting someone else. It's helpful to remember that your friend or loved one is likely in a place in life which wasn't at all what they had planned. Being in the position of needing the support of others can be a stretch for them, making them feel uncomfortable, undeserving, inadequate, or weak. It can sometimes push them to emotional extremes and lead them to take out their frustrations on the very people who are trying to help them. If you anticipate it and see it for what it is, you will be better able to handle it.

If the supported person suddenly reaches their limit of irritation or exasperation, they'll probably aim their annoyance at whomever is nearby. In most cases, you must understand that it's *not about you*. That said, in addition to attempting to understand what their underlying issue(s) might be, you as the care-giver will also want to put healthy boundaries in place for yourself.

Again, let's start with a few examples of unhealthy boundaries:

- You disregard the needs, expectations, and preferences of your friend or loved one
- You express disapproval for the cause of their current circumstances
- You decide on their best course of action to mend or mitigate their problem
- You expect them to follow your advice and rules
- You disrespect their home, property, or personal space
- You feel as though their success and happiness are now your responsibility
- You feel as though you need to save or fix them
- You complain regularly about the imposition their problem has become on you and your life

Now, some healthy alternatives:

- You show respect and compassion for the person you are supporting *regardless of the reason they need your support*
- You help them maintain their dignity and remember they are first and foremost human beings, like you
- You give them frequent opportunities to express

what kind of support they most want from you

- You consider their needs, preferences, and schedules before deciding on a plan of action
- You give them privacy and autonomy; you ask before proceeding in a new or different direction
- You offer opinions and suggestions only when they have been requested
- You touch others only with their permission
- You respect the choices they make
- You try to look at the situation from their point of view
- You see yourself as their helper, not their boss
- You stay out of their mail, medicine cabinet, personal business, and belongings
- You show them respect when they say "no"
- You let them decide when they are or are not up to having visitors

On the occasions when your support is needed by someone you love or care about, having a healthy attitude toward everyone's personal boundaries will help to ensure that your loving relationship continues well beyond the time you are supporting them.

Recommended Resources
Here are some on-line resources that can be helpful when you are giving or receiving support:

- **Lotsa Helping Hands**. This organization offers a free mobile app to easily organize help for someone in need and provide a central place to coordinate meals and help for friends and family. www.lotsa-helpinghands.com

- **Care Calendar**. This website's motto is "bringing communities together to care for loved ones." Their purpose is to "help organize meals and other help for families during a time of illness, recovery or a life changing event, such as the birth of a baby or death of a family member." When help is needed, all you need to do is list your need and then family and friends can sign up to help. www.carecalendar.org

- **Caring Bridge**. It can be exhausting for someone to keep all of their friends and family updated on their current condition or situation. This website helps make that task easier by providing a place to share news, updates, photos, and videos with those they want to keep in the loop. It also works as a way to let them know you need support and how they can support you. www.caringbridge.org

- **Cancer Support Community**. Similar to Caring Bridge, this website "exists to easily connect cancer patients and caregivers with friends and family in order to reduce stress, anxiety, and isolation." Their goal is to "help you find hope, regain control, document your journey, receive social, emotional, and practical support from friends and family. They also have discussion boards covering a wide range of relevant topics. www.mylifeline.org

- **Family Medical Leave Act**: Detailed information regarding the Family Medical Leave Act. This site will help your support network know about federal laws that help family members support one another while keeping their jobs intact. www.dol.gov/whd/fmla

CHAPTER FIFTEEN
The Power of Words

I came to understand the power of words when I was a child. My father taught me to always be careful when I spoke because there was power in every word. I learned that just the simple act of conversing with someone could actually be introducing subtle suggestions into their brain, and could have a huge impact on them in both positive and negative ways. In recent years, as a medical massage therapist—or *myotherapist*—I often see firsthand how my words affect my clients and patients.

Most of us don't realize that our muscles can be directly affected by words. How? Our muscles are controlled by our brains, and our brains are affected by what they hear. I have helped people stand straighter just with words of encouragement alone.

But words can also direct our focus. When facing hard

truths, we have a choice in where we place our focus and whose words we listen to. During my treatment, when some people visiting me focused on my cancer, I felt the pain and therefore remained focused on the disease I had with all its potential side effects and outcomes. I realized how bad that was for me, so I stopped encouraging those folks to stop by and exercised more intention when with friends and family. That way I could avoid those negatives and begin focusing on the positives instead.

How Our Words Affect Others

On my last day of seventh grade, Ms. Haskin, an English teacher in my junior high, wrote something in my yearbook that has stayed with me for all the years since. Rather than the usual, meaningless platitudes like "stay as sweet as you are" or "good luck in all your endeavors," Ms. Haskin said, "It's been a pleasure knowing you and of course it doesn't end here. Set your goals high, Robert, and make your dreams come true. I'll be excited to hear about your high school and college experiences!"

I remember feeling a warm rush of excitement about my future when I read her message to me. It was almost as if she was pulling a curtain aside to reveal an unforeseen world of possibilities. Her inspiring words still resonate in my thoughts these many years later.

Our selective memory usually helps us reduce the trivial clutter from idle conversations so the words that are impactful can remain fresh in our thoughts for years to come. If you ask me what so-and-so said a week ago, or what I might have casually said to my mom on the phone, I probably wouldn't be able to recall. If my doctor calls with the results of a blood test, believe me—I pay attention. In addition to words that have vital importance, the kinds of words that stick tend to be either loving, encouraging, complimentary, and motivating, or hurtful, damaging, demeaning, and cruel. Our words can create emotional wounds or they can help to heal emotional wounds, and the effects can last a lifetime.

I have also learned the painful lesson that saying the same thing to two different people can elicit two different responses. Even our intonation can impact how our words are heard. For example, saying to someone, "Nice hair," can return a response of, "Thanks—just got it cut!" Or, it can return a less confident response, such as, "What's *wrong* with my hair?" Keep your audience in mind and be careful choosing your words.

Several times a year I hear from therapists who have attended my classes, who want to thank me for something encouraging I said to them years earlier. They can recount the conversations verbatim as if they happened yesterday and tell me how my words affected them. Without knowing it, my words of encouragement had become an investment in their futures. Just as Dr. Stephen Bayles was encouraged from something I had said a year earlier and helped him work through his fears, the things you say can be a comforting, healing salve on the hearts and minds of others going through a period of adversity. At the same time, you may unintentionally say something hurtful which will remain in someone's 'baggage' for years to come.

Depending on circumstances, it can be a real challenge to know what kinds of things it's okay to say to someone who is experiencing adversity—and the kinds of things it's better not to say. Some people find the skill so daunting that they end up not being there at all for a friend or loved one in their time of need, simply because they don't know what to say.

But how do you know what is the right or wrong thing to say? How do you comfort or encourage your friend or loved one but not add to his burden? By saying, "You're going to beat this!" to a cancer patient may sound to you like you're offering encouragement, but now the patient could be feeling the pressure of having to perform. If he ends up not beating the adversity, did he not try hard enough? If your sister is going through incredible hardship around her finances, it serves no purpose to tell her how hard it is for you to see her in this predicament.

First, keep in mind that while it may scare you, sadden you, worry you, or anger you, *it's not about you.* Second, venting your fears and your emotional distress to her is misdirected; she already has enough to worry about. Don't be selfish and add to someone's burden. Be sure to think about how what you say could affect them.

Clinical psychologist Susan Silk, co-author of a 2013 op-ed piece in the Los Angeles Times entitled *How Not to Say the Wrong Thing*[35], describes what she refers to as the Ring Theory, which provides general guidance regarding whom you should simply be comforting, and whom it's okay to express your concerns to. She suggests taking a piece of paper and writing the name of the individual going through adversity, right in the center of the paper, with a small circle around it. Then, draw a somewhat larger circle around that and fill in the name of the next closest person, such as a spouse or parent. The next circle

---

[35] Silk, S., Goldman, B. (2013, April 7). How Not to Say the Wrong Thing. Los Angeles Times. Retrieved from https://www.latimes.com/opinion/op-ed/la-xpm-2013-apr-07-la-oe-0407-silk-ring-theory-20130407-story.html

might have their child or best friend. The process continues as you add each ring, or layer, and include those who are less and less involved. In most cases, you'd include siblings in a more inward circle, for example, while old college friends would go in an outer circle. By doing this, you are constructing a visual representation of relationship proximity. The theory is this: Whoever is in the center ring can say anything to anyone. They have an excuse to complain, cry, swear, or behave childishly to whomever they want. The people whose names are in the larger circles can do the same thing, but never to those in the rings that are smaller than theirs. Those in the smaller circles need comfort and support rather than words of concern, pressure, or emotional stress.

Things You Should Never Say to Someone Navigating Adversity

It takes forethought and mental preparation to know what to say to someone who is experiencing a significant health or personal crisis, such as a life-threatening disease or the loss of a close loved one. So many of us intend to encourage someone with our words but end up inflicting emotional wounds instead.

Here are some examples of things you should never say, and why:

- **"You're going to be fine."** Why? Nobody truly knows that for sure; it sounds superficial and meaningless.

- **"Everything happens for a reason."** Why? Although good may ultimately come from the situation, thinking God gave you cancer isn't comforting and doesn't align with the sacred texts of most faiths.

- **"That's why I never use antiperspirant. It gives you cancer, you know."** Why? We shouldn't give advice on how to avoid cancer or offer our insights on what must have caused it. Our bodies all respond differently to different things, and basically, it can be the luck of the draw.

- **"What do you need me to do for you?"** Why? For someone who's in the throes of adversity, even the energy expended while trying to think of what you can do can be exhausting. It is very likely they don't even know what they need—so don't make them think about it. Instead, go ahead and straighten up their house. Do some cleaning or laundry. Bring them a good book or a stack of magazines or offer to read to them.

- **"Tell me all of the details! How did it happen? Did it hurt? Can I see it?"** Why? They've likely been asked those painful questions before, and each time they are forced to retell it, they have to *relive every detail* of the dreadful moment. If they want you to know personal details, they will tell you in their own time.

- **"It's not that bad. You've got insurance."** Why? Making this type of statement is dismissing the immeasurable impact of the event—the time, expense, and inconvenience of getting back to normal again, and minimizing the losses incurred, disruption to their lives, and potential PTSD from the event itself.

- **"You have to stop eating sugar!"** Why? Don't give nutritional advice. The theories you've heard or read about are often baseless and unproven. Plus, certain foods or supplements can adversely affect any ongoing treatments. Different bodies respond to things differently. Finally, you don't want to make someone feel they are to blame for their misfortune.

- **"Any one of us could get hit by a car in the crosswalk tomorrow."** Why? It's true; anyone could. Don't diminish what they are experiencing now by talking about what could happen to someone else later.

- **"Miracles happen!"** Why? This colloquialism can result in a range of responses. The patient most often hears the unspoken subtext: "You're going to *need* a miracle."

- **"It happened to your uncle but his was way worse."** Why? Making comparisons to other people's experiences is meaningless and dismissive.

- **"I'm just too busy to visit. Sorry."** Why? Don't avoid a friend or loved one because you won't know what to say or because you're uncomfortable being around someone who's been through a catastrophe. They need you. Be there for them. It's not about you.

What *Can* You Say to Comfort Someone Amidst Adversity?

When in doubt regarding what you can say or do when you're talking to someone having a rough time, keep in mind these five basic guidelines:

- **Be positive.** You don't have to point out all the negatives; they've likely already gone there themselves.

- **Be genuine.** Don't feign concern or make meaningless comments. No one has time for that.

- **Remain in contact throughout their journey, recovery, and aftermath**. Don't be just a fair-weather friend.

- **Be sensitive in your actions and words.** Don't bring a deck of cards to someone who's just broken his arm.

- **Don't make their ordeal about you.** It's *not*. It happened or is happening to *them.*

- **Demonstrate that you care by your actions and not just your words**. What you *do* speaks volumes.

The good news is, there actually are some things that are safe to say when someone's having a significant health issue or in the aftermath of a catastrophic event. Here are some to help you get started:

- **"This sucks!"** Why? It's true. Showing empathy is always better than sympathy.

- **"Your strength is impressive."** Why? Words of encouragement are important.

- **"Did you watch last weekend's Saturday Night**

Live?" Why? Talking about things other than sickness and adversity can be a very welcome distraction. It can also help to normalize the moment for both of you.

- **"We can talk about whatever you'd like, and if you need to vent your anger and complain, I'm here to listen."** Why? Simply showing up and being there for your friend is powerful. Giving them the opportunity to talk about what they want to is an even greater gift.

- **"I will be coming to visit next week in the afternoon. Would Tuesday or Wednesday work better for you?"** Why? Asking if they would like you to visit can leave some people in a quandary because they don't want to be a bother or a burden on others. Don't ask if—ask *when*. Then, bring them some kind of fun treat that they haven't asked for.

What to Say to Someone Who's Lost Spouse, Friend, or Family Member

After a life partner, family member, or close friend passes away, those who were in their inner circle will go through various states of emotional responses. Despite having good intentions and wanting to comfort them, we can sometimes say things that end up intensifying their sadness or inflicting unnecessary pain rather than providing comfort. Allen Roth, who talked to me about the loss of his daughter, spoke about the emotional rollercoaster bereaved parents experience after the death of their child. His insights apply equally to anyone, regardless of whom they've lost.

"People either went away for not knowing what to say," Allen recalled, "or they made things worse with their poor responses. It was hurtful to be told such things as, 'She is in a better place,' 'It was God's plan,' 'It was meant to be,' 'Everything happens for a reason,' or, 'You'll get over it in time.' Avoid making statements beginning with the phrase, 'At least …,' such as 'At least you still have your other child.' Others will make a child's passing about them. Some will draw close and be there while others will pull away, not knowing what to do."

When I asked Allen what you *can* say to someone who has just lost a child, his answer was, "What I say is, 'From this day forward, there will come a time when life will become worth living again,' and they look at me in disbelief, because no one believes that at first. And I say, 'Don't believe me, but hear the words … there is hope. Carry those words with you, and over time, they will become real for you.'"

CHAPTER SIXTEEN
Bitter or Better?

I was asked recently if I feel I've emerged from my cancer-related experiences *bitter* or *better*. It was a good question and it got me thinking. Had all that adversity left me angry and resentful, or was it the impetus to becoming a better version of the man I had been before?

As I have joked in the past, life is basically a death sentence. Our bodies are only capable of living for a finite period of time. Some of us will die from heart disease or an accident, while others will pull the cancer card. The fact is, every one of us has cancer cells in our bodies, but normally, our immune systems defend us. It's like a *cancer lottery*. Some of us will get it; most of us won't. I got it. So, how did it impact me?

With a few exceptions, I have never really been a bitter person. The few times I have been resentful about something, the emotions that came from holding on to the bitterness were so toxic that I had to let go of them entirely in order to restore my emotional well-being.

Someone once told me that holding on to bitterness and resentment is like drinking poison and hoping it will kill some-one else. It's true! Simply put, being bitter is a waste of time. First, we compromise the quality of our lives when our bitter-ness manifests itself as stress-related health issues. More im-portantly, we spend what's left of our lives being miserable when we could have lived our lives joyously and been a bless-ing to others.

Ironically, bitterness is typically an easy emotion to spot in another person while *better* isn't always clearly obvious. The question of being *better* is not referring to a state of physicality, but a state of mind and balance in life. *Better* is relative to each person as well as each person's beliefs. What better means for most people, however, is a change from their place of negativity into one with healthy thoughts, healthy habits, feeling content-ment, use of healthy coping mechanisms, and having a realistic perspective on past events. How do we get to a place of being better? Great question.

In the past two decades, Dr. Michael Linden, a German psychiatrist, along with others in the field of psychiatry, has been conducting studies on a frequently encountered condi-tion they refer to as *Post Traumatic Embitterment Disorder*, or PTED[36]. It is not the same thing as *Post Traumatic Stress Disor-der*, although people dealing with PTED often suffer from

---

[36] Linden M. Posttraumatic Embitterment Disorder. Psychother Psychosom. 2003;72(4):195-202. doi:10.1159/000070783

PTSD. It is a condition with which an individual's anger and bitterness can ultimately interfere with their life and eventually, even their health[37].

It just doesn't make sense to me to hold on to negative feelings like that, for whatever reasons. I know too many people who do just that, and it's not healthy for them or for anyone around them. I actually find it difficult to spend time with them and I definitely don't want to be "that guy" myself. I prefer to be positive, feel positive, and spread positivity to the people around me.

What's the answer? How do we face unfathomable trauma and not end up bitter? It would be easy to flippantly say, "Just choose to be!" That's about as effective as the old directive to "just say no to drugs." Although being better comes down to a series of cognitive choices, *choosing* is only the first step in the journey. It is much easier said than done for most people.

As countless cognitive behavioral therapists will attest, our thoughts, which originate in our brains, create emotions, which are the *physical sensations* of our thoughts. Good thoughts are healthy for our bodies, and bad thoughts are unhealthy for our bodies. The bottom line is this: how we *think*, affects how we *feel*, which affects how we *act*. All three can influence and affect each other.

It might seem like the process appears as though it's *paint-by-numbers-psychology*, but it sort of is. When a situation or event takes place, we use our thoughts to interpret it, and our

---

[37] Kubzansky, L. D., Sparrow, D., Jackson, B., Cohen, S., Weiss, S. T., & Wright, R. J. (2006). Angry breathing: A prospective study of hostility and lung function in the Normative Aging Study. *Thorax*, *61*(10), 863–868. https://doi.org/10.1136/thx.2005.050971

thoughts create an emotion. If we don't like the emotion we are feeling, we go back and identify which thought needs to be changed, replace the thought with a better one, and end up changing our emotion, which will eventually lead to making better choices in how we act.

We can spend years—decades even—seething with bitterness and anger towards someone else for their role in tragic events. It's easy to overlook our own imperfections yet hold other people accountable for theirs, especially if that imperfection takes away what we treasure most in the world.

Several of the people I interviewed for this book were parents who, tragically, had lost children due to the neglectful actions (or inactions) of others. They have continued living with extreme pain, anguish, and rage, many years after their children's passing. The story shared with me by one family, in particular, was especially devastating.

The Kelloggs

Before the 2008 recession, Bryson and Nancy Kellogg were doing well and living a good life. They had a successful business, three wonderful children, and they had recently moved into their dream home. When the recession began to affect his business, Bryson missed his first mortgage payment and their marriage began to crumble. Eventually, he had to move out of the house.

"I had a really hard time after we separated," he told me. "My wife got full custody of our kids and I missed seeing them.

I was grieving the loss of regularly spending time with them because of the restrictive visitation schedule that was put into place."

Over the next year, Bryson's business started to improve again. He allowed himself to make plans and feel optimistic for the future, until his phone rang one night. It was a police officer from his wife's community. The words he heard were devastating.

"Mr. Kellogg, I am at your ex-wife's house—it's fully engulfed in flames." Numbed by the police officer's words, Bryson quickly got dressed and was on the road in minutes. On the way, while listening to his emergency services radio scanner, he heard the police dispatcher calling for a chaplain. His heart sank.

When he arrived, Nancy was in the front yard, fully dressed and unscathed, but the police soon confirmed every parent's worst nightmare: all three of their children had died in the fire.

Although a police investigation ultimately cleared her of wrongdoing, the fact was that Nancy's actions had indeed resulted in the children's death. Her careless housekeeping had created a fire hazard, she had allowed their smoke alarm to go defunct, and she had been drinking heavily the night of the fire. Bryson is understandably angry, and he knows who he is angry with. He also misses his kids.

"That was the night my life ended," he told me. "You're torn simultaneously by a desire to run away from everything and forget and a desire to hold on so tight that you never lose anything. But the *loneliness* ... the loneliness is the hardest thing when you are suffering. You can't prepare for this kind of loss, and you don't get over it. It becomes a part of you. At some point, you simply have to adapt and accept that you are not the same person you were before."

Today, while continuing to process his incalculable loss, Bryson is remarried, working hard, and learning how to navigate his new life. He has moved forward from his tragedy and honors his three children with a monument engraved with their names at the school they attended.

Regardless of your right to feel angry and bitter, you have a choice. You can choose to be bitter *or* better as you emerge from the challenges you have experienced. Choosing to be better may not be instinctual for you, particularly if your bitterness is bottled up and focused on someone who is to blame. Your pain will likely fade away if you choose to forgive even those you may have previously deemed *unforgivable.*

Tears ran down my cheeks as I watched a courtroom scene on the news in the Fall of 2019. In an act of unconditional love and forgiveness, 18-year-old Brandt Jean was asking a judge if he could hug Amber Guyger, a former Dallas police officer, who had just been convicted in the shooting death of his older brother[38].

In his impact statement directed toward Amber, Brandt said, "I'm not gonna say I hope you rot and die like my brother did. I forgive you, and I know if you go to God and ask Him, He will forgive you. I love you just like anyone else, and I want the best for you, just as my brother would."

He then turned to the judge and asked, "Can I give her a

---

[38] Da Salva, C. (2019, October 3). 'Forgiveness' is trending after moment Botham Jean's brother hugged police officer who killed him and told her: 'I don't even want you to go to jail'. Newsweek. Retrieved from https://www.newsweek.com/botham-jean-brother-bryant-offers-forgiveness-hug-amber-guyger-dallas-1462868

hug, please?" The judge allowed it, and the people in the court-room looked on in amazement, as did millions of viewers who were watching the news across the country. The miracle of for-giveness is the peace that results from letting go of hurt and pain.

I recall one other time when forgiveness had a strong and healing effect. When I was in intensive care following my sur-gery, my ex-wife, Debbie—my girls' mother—came and visited me in the hospital. After talking for about an hour, we agreed to forgive one another for all the hurts we had been holding on to for so long. Her visit and our frank conversation did much to clear the air. As Debbie was about to leave, she put her hand on my shoulder and leaned down and whispered, "I love you" in my ear. That was a memorable moment for me, realizing the powerful impact of true forgiveness.

We have a choice to forgive or to hold on to the negative emotions which can halt our emotional growth. Forgiveness is not for the benefit of the person we are forgiving, but for the person doing the forgiving, because it releases us from the shackles of bitterness.

CHAPTER SEVENTEEN
In Search of Meaning

True adversity can be a scary place to be mentally. Those of us going through the experience are often coping alone. We've been caught off guard. No one had sought our permission, nor has anyone helped us know what our next steps should be. We frankly don't know how to think, what to do, or who else has been impacted. Before trying to answer any questions about moving forward, most of us find ourselves searching for the answer to one simple question: *What meaning can I find in this experience that will help me understand why and how it happened?*

The desire to find the meaning, the answer to "why?" rises up in most of us. Some people will seek out answers from their spiritual leaders, some from a guru on a mountain top, and others from their drinking buddies. To come to an understanding of the *meaning of our adversity*, we need to begin with our beliefs about the *meaning of life*.

Some philosophers believe life is meaningless, and that our tiny presence in the cosmos is insignificant and without purpose. This way of thinking is defined as the theory of *existential nihilism,* which essentially is the belief that there is no meaning to life, nothing is good or bad, there is no god, and values and morals are meaningless. Those who hold these beliefs won't find meaning behind their adversity because to them there is no meaning. It's neither good nor bad. For those of us who are not existential nihilists, we can look deeper.

From the outset, I am not convinced every type of adversity inherently has meaning attached to it. When the six-inch steel bolt I drove over punctured through both my car tire and the rim of the wheel, I wasn't racking my brain to find meaning. Did it mean I should change careers so I could work with steel bolts? No. Was it a sign that driving a car is bad for the climate and I should get a bus pass instead? Again, no.

When I spoke with my insurance claim adjuster, she said, "Mr. Haase, you ran over an object in the road. It didn't jump up and attack your car or fall off of a contractor's truck. It was there, and you chose to drive over it rather than around it. It was your responsibility to look for road hazards, Mr. Haase. Your claim for a new tire and wheel is denied." What meaning did she impart to me? Clearly, I needed a new eyeglass prescription—at least that's the meaning the adjuster got out of it. We can't always see what lies ahead. Adversity will come eventually, but it doesn't mean there is *meaning* attached to it. *How we think* and *how we respond* to adversity is what brings meaning for us as individuals.

When a group of friends are involved in an accident where their SUV veered off the road and crashed into a tree, each of them will interpret the event differently based on their belief system, and how it lines up compared to their previous experiences. The driver believes it was a sign he should go to rehab to stop drinking, another friend believes it was a sign he should run for mayor to get the street lighting improved, and another believes it happened because they weren't supposed to attend the concert they were driving to. The tree was simply there.

Angry at God?

A friend asked me this past week about my attitude after my experiences with adversity. He said, "Answer me, honestly—*seriously*, why aren't you mad?" I have been asked that question more than once. When horrible things happen, people often get angry and ask, "Why would a 'loving God' allow this to happen?" They get furious at God because He didn't keep "bad" from happening in this world.

We, humans, have free will—the ability to make choices that affect our future. Our choices have consequences, with each choice setting into motion chains of events with far-reaching ripple effects, which culminate in both positive and negative outcomes. Yet we blame God even though a negative outcome ultimately was the result of decisions made by others. Accidents happen as do chains of events that lead to peril.

Remember that Carrie Underwood song, "Jesus Take the Wheel"? The reality is, if we genuinely want to keep bad things from happening on this earth, that is *literally* what would have to happen. Unless I want to give up my free will, I cannot blame

God for the bad things that happen in my life and my world. Let me give you an analogy: Let's say you have been craving a big, greasy burger, so you get into your car and find the nearest burger joint. Meanwhile, God knows your greasy burger habit will lead to cardiovascular disease, and suddenly, the steering wheel overrides your input, and your car drives itself to a *vegan* restaurant. Would you be angry? Given a choice, would you be willing to give up the freedom of free will? Do you *actually* want God to take the wheel? We want free will yet still blame the negative consequences of our choices on God.

A parent might blame God because their daughter is dead, but not be accountable for demonstrating a life of alcohol-related mishaps in front of their daughter, who eventually thought it would be okay to drive under the influence.

Ultimately, an event's meaning is what you decide it is. Perhaps we shouldn't spend time searching for an event's underlying meaning and instead come to terms with the *reason* something happened and then focus on the blessings adversity has left us with.

I Must Have Done *Something* to Deserve This

After receiving my cancer diagnosis, people sometimes said things to me that were both hurtful and untrue. One well-meaning visitor said, "It must be because there is sin in your life." Another told me "There is cancer in your tongue because there is something that you aren't confessing—a truth you haven't spoken," and another said, "There is someone you haven't forgiven—you need to forgive. *You have cancer because of your unforgiving heart!*" The fact is, none of those things was true.

Bad things happen to good people, period.

Here are some other beliefs that people frequently go to when trying to find meaning from adversity:

- I must have caused it with my own actions/choices.
- I didn't appreciate what I had while I had it.
- I haven't always been a nice person; I've mistreated others.
- It was bound to happen; my life was going too smoothly before.
- I've always had it too easy; I had to pay my dues eventually.
- It's my mother's fault for something she must have done while pregnant with me.
- I shouldn't have been _____ in the first place.
- I haven't been a good (<u>son/husband/brother/friend</u>).
- I haven't paid enough attention to God.

These false beliefs are not why this has happened to you. The sooner you let go of these ideas, the sooner you will be able to move forward in your life and recognize the actual gifts the experience has brought.

"I Am Blessed"

Several years before my own cancer diagnosis, I was in New York City for a training course on massage treatments for cancer patients. On the last day of the training, we accompanied the lead therapist on her rounds, meeting her cancer patients along the way. Toward the end of her shift, we approached the room of an elderly gentleman whose nurse was willing to share some of his health history. She told us he was recovering from recent surgery that had removed part of his throat, and he was in a great deal of pain.

As we entered the room, the nurse asked him, "So, how are we doing today, Mr. Washington?"

It took a few seconds for him to clear his throat and position himself so he could answer her question. Finally, with a gentle smile and a raspy, strained voice, he said, simply, "I am blessed."

Of course, I had no idea at the time how the elderly man's words would exemplify an attitude of gratitude and blessing. I decided then that, should I ever find myself in a similar situation, I would emulate his attitude and look for the blessings.

Occasionally, when I look at myself in the mirror these days, I still just see a man with a permanently disfigured body living in the aftermath of cancer. The words Mr. Washington spoke nearly two decades ago will ring fresh in my ears—words that now have a great deal of personal meaning. I smile and know, despite my circumstances, I am blessed!

The Gifts of Adversity

Going through surgery and cancer treatment remains one of the most difficult and harrowing experiences I have ever faced. My 240-pound body lost nearly 90 pounds, and at a gaunt 151 pounds, I wasn't sure if I would make it. On the upside, the gifts and lessons I received along the way—gifts I might not have gotten otherwise—were powerful and invaluable, and have helped me navigate my life ever since.

Through my experiences and interactions with others, I learned to:

- Receive and accept unconditional love
- Receive and accept help and kindness from others
- Recognize and confront my own mortality
- Be comfortable when experiencing humility
- Remind myself things could always be worse
- Be patient. Still working on that one occasionally
- Be more empathetic and compassionate towards others
- Choose an outward orientation in place of a self-centered focus
- Reconsider my priorities and perspectives
- Experience joy regardless of hardship.
- Live my life with gratitude
- Search for and act on my life's purpose

The obstacles that force us to change our course of direction might be the greatest gift of all, because they can lead us to an even better destination than the one we were heading toward. We all know the direction we'd like to be going. If we allow them, our adverse experiences can bring clarity and insight to the direction our future takes.

INDEX

Index

M

N

Index

Index

threshold 35, 44–45, 100, 197
tongue 16–18, 20–25, 28, 30–31, 35, 70, 87, 141, 186, 197, 199
trauma 13–14, 59, 73, 78, 88, 92–93, 111, 134, 177–178, 197
treatment 7–8, 13–14, 29, 32, 38–41, 93, 100, 106, 115, 120, 126, 135–
    138, 140, 142–144, 153, 159, 167, 172, 187–188, 197
tree 44, 46–47, 108, 127, 185, 197

V

vaccine 99, 145, 197
value 70, 76, 84, 88, 90, 120, 197
values 64, 184, 197

W

wait 13, 20, 24, 29–31, 34, 197
Washington 6, 12, 75, 111, 188, 197
weak 14, 29, 41, 72, 118, 141, 147, 153, 161, 197
wheelchair 71–73, 198
wife 3, 7, 33, 52, 62, 68, 75, 80, 123, 126, 138–139, 144, 179–180, 198
wisdom 45–46, 77, 82, 86, 117, 198
word 5, 7–8, 18, 29–35, 37, 39, 47, 89, 114, 117, 120, 129, 133–134, 141,
    143, 153, 157, 166–168, 170, 173, 175, 180, 188, 198
work 4, 8, 10–15, 21–23, 28, 35, 37, 53, 55, 57–58, 61, 64, 66, 69–71, 76–
    80, 85, 88, 92–93, 95–96, 100, 102–103, 106, 109, 111, 113, 123,
    129, 131, 136, 139, 141, 143, 145, 148, 154, 164, 168, 174, 181,
    184, 189, 198–199
worry 21, 27, 36, 91, 131, 135, 149, 152, 155, 169, 198
wyanne 87, 198

X

Xingwei 38, 198

Y

yoga 84–85, 198

SPEAKER INFORMATION

Robert B. Haase has been a speaker and educator for over 20 years and presents to audiences with experience, energy, and intensity of purpose. After facing numerous overwhelming and life-changing adversities, he has refocused his purpose on giving encouragement and tools to help others navigate through adversities of their own. In a year's time, Robert went through a divorce, was diagnosed with cancer, lost his home, as well as the vocational school he had worked to build from the ground up over the previous decade.

After over a dozen surgeries, Robert lost the left half of his tongue to stop a fast-growing cancer from taking his life in 2013. In the years since, Robert has worked diligently to regain the articulate voice he has since relied on to inspire audiences throughout the United States.

In the years since, Robert has expanded his expertise in the area of facing adversity through his interviews with hundreds of people who have faced a broad spectrum of adversities.

Robert B. Haase, speaking before an audience in Spokane, WA.

Content Covered in Robert's Stories:
- Navigating Constant Change
- Shedding the Victim Mentality
- Realizing Perspective is a Choice
- Using Change to Find New Purpose
- Purposeful Steps Towards Building Resilience
- Mastering Adversity
- Inspiring Compassionate Leadership
- Looking at Obstacles as New Opportunities
- Revealing the Power of the Human Spirit
- Living a Life of Thankfulness
- Finding Fortitude to Grow in Courage

To inquire about securing Robert's speaking services, send an email to events@roberthaase.com, or call (360) 810-3641. Additional information can be found on our website at www.notwhatyouhadplanned.org.

Speaker Information

www.ingramcontent.com/pod-product-compliance
Lightning Source LLC
LaVergne TN
LVHW011225080426
835509LV00005B/324